In Search of a Past

In Search of a Past

The Rearing of an English Gentleman
1933-1945

Ronald Fraser

NEW YORK *Atheneum* 1984

For Mark and Jessica

'In the artist of all kinds I think one can detect an inherent dilemma, which belongs to the co-existence of two trends: the urgent need to communicate and the still more urgent need not to be found.'

—D.W. Winnicott

Acknowledgements

Without the help of a great many people this book could not have been written. I wish especially to thank all those who worked at the Manor House and who, a quarter of a century later, welcomed me into their homes to recall their experiences. Recorded pseudonymously here, their memories allowed me my first access to the past. But I also owe them an apology: for reasons that, as they will see, lie at the heart of the book, it could not be written until many years later.

I also wish to thank Sir John and Lady Figgess, and Drs. David and Audrey Price for their kindness in allowing me to revisit my past.

As the reader will note, I owe a special debt of gratitude to P, the psychoanalyst whose endeavours made it finally possible to write the book, and who offered many invaluable suggestions; a similar debt is due to my brother, Colin Fraser, who not only shared his memories with me but provided numerous insights into the past.

Finally, I wish to thank Jane Mills, Francis Mulhern, W.L. Webb and Neil Belton for their encouragement and helpful criticisms at different stages of the writing.

Contents

We

The road stretches ahead under a grey summer sky. The old man's mind is starred, a shattered windscreen of opaque desires and memories. Where does this road go? He looks without seeing, or sees without recognizing, the distant white house, hull-down on the edge of the flatlands below the fir-crested hill. Have I any friends? In the silence his eyes fix on the road again, and the Manor disappears behind Amnersfield wood.

There's a long silence, and then I say:
'I remember . . . Ah yes, returning after twenty-five years, how white and clear the house stood out from a distance. I could see the brick chimneys and old roofs at the rear and the slate-roofed tower at the front, my eyes took in the whole house for the first time. It was an unusually luminous afternoon, perhaps that explains it, for even the flatlands seemed to shimmer. And above them, like a liner on an empty sea, the Manor floated serenely clear . . .

'I got back in the car and drove on with mounting expectation. When I reached the house everything would at last fall into place. But then – and this is what I was trying to say before – with each turn of the approaching road the view began to lose clarity. The closer I got the further the house receded behind walls, out-buildings, tall trees until, driving past, there was only a fleeting glimpse of white beyond the stable yard . . .'

I paused, glancing at P. in the chair under the window. His tanned face was impassive, his light grey summer suit immaculate. I looked for his eyes but they remained turned down. Did he never look at you? Or speak? . . .

'All right, it's only a metaphor, I know, but it has a reality. Because, when I walked to the back gate, I saw that my eyes hadn't deceived me, that the old roofs and chimneys were hidden from the road by the stables and head gardener's cottage. So, too, was the front – by a thick laurel hedge. Along the road an old fence shut out the view, and then as always the front drive curved through a mass of evergreens to an invisible front door. As a last resort, I walked down the church path: the tall yew hedge Bert used to clip concluded the matter. The place remained impenetrable, enclosed by walls of every sort. And that's how it has always been . . . '

I waited expectantly. P. said nothing. Disconcerted, I began to regret having taken this step. Other psychoanalysts were surely more forthcoming, I thought, taking comfort in the knowledge that this was only a preliminary meeting without commitment on either side.

Again I tried: 'It's always been like that – either confined behind them in childhood or shut out later by those walls. I can't get back . . . ' Seeing his mouth twitch, as though he were smiling to himself, I stopped. There was a silence and then I said: 'Look, I've spent ten years trying to dispose of the past by committing it to paper. Uselessly, of course, otherwise I wouldn't be here.'

'Do you believe the past can be disposed of?'

His voice was rather soft, middle to upper-middle class, I guessed, but there was no way of telling for sure, and his eyes were blue and rather hard. For some reason his question pleased me.

'Certainly I do. Don't you?'

'What exactly are you hoping for?'

'Mmm . . . To consign – no, to recreate an uncertain past . . . '

' . . . '

'With sufficient certainty to put it behind me.'

He lowered his eyes again.

'But it eludes me', I went on undeterred. 'Those walls are inside me, I feel . . . Or rather, perhaps, it's something like split vision.'

'What do you mean?' he asked, looking up.

'It's as though I go on seeing each of those worlds with separate eyes. No perspective. It's not surprising, perhaps, because there were two worlds, two houses within those same walls . . . '

Two Manors, under different roofs, I explained, the old at the rear, a place of small, pleasant rooms with bulging beams and walls thick enough to withstand a siege where servants, nanny and children lived; and the superimposed and imposing new Manor at the front, which belonged to the parents. The large Victorian dining and drawing rooms, separated by a dark hall, the smoking room and the sweeping stairs which led to the main bedroom, guest-rooms and the tower were semi-alien territory where I ventured with caution. 'Not that there was anything very strange about that, given the time and place, I suppose. I belonged without yet belonging . . .'

Anticipating a dialogue, I looked at him but his eyes had vanished again. I glanced at my watch: another ten minutes and I'd be leaving. Ah well, a step down another false path, it couldn't be helped. Unexpectedly, I found myself fixed in a hard, blue-eyed gaze.

'I was wondering why your memories are all of the house rather than of the people.'

'I was going to come to them . . . Now that you ask, they reflect the same closeness and distance as the house.'

He nodded, I thought, and I took it as a sign to continue: the immediate foreground was shared by Ilse, forever starchily uniformed and loving, to whom I was attached by immemorial bonds; and Bert, who was eternally digging the garden and pulling funny faces from beneath his cocked trilby to make me laugh. At one remove there was Carvell, grave-faced and silent, mucking out the hunters in the stables with a hissing sound that went through me like a chill wind; and outside in the stable yard, old Dolcie stomping back and forth, muttering to herself: sometimes close, at other times far away in her madness. Over at the pantry window, in his black butler's coat, Johnson was always a distant figure, slipping away from a small boy's silent gaze; while in the kitchen Marie was little more than a voice shouting angrily, heard from afar because Ilse didn't let me go in there often. Upstairs, dusting and sweeping, Eileen and Doris in their blue housemaid's uniform, were close at hand but I knew that I mustn't spend long talking to them.

'That was one world of varying closeness. More distantly, as though in another world, I can see my mother, Janey, in top hat and veil, mounted side-saddle on her dappled grey mare, and the back of my father's red coat as they left for the hunt. It would be dark before they returned. Their comings and goings seemed to obey laws as unfamiliar as those of the universe; the world of the servants was permanent and familiar.'

'This was all pre-war?'

'Yes. We came to the Manor in 1933 when I was two-and-a-half. Ilse came from Germany with us. I thought I had explained that at the beginning.'

'Yes,' he said, 'I just wanted to be clear.' For a moment I thought he smiled. 'Your descriptions seem clear enough.'

'Writers lie to tell the truth. They have to, don't they?'

He said nothing, and I felt I had gone too far. Then: 'Is that what you feel – that you've been lying?'

'No. Selective vision gives many writers insight, I know. But for me, it's like looking through the wrong end of a telescope. I can't find the myth or lie that brings the past into focus. So, ten years ago, I stopped looking for one. I set out instead to discover how the others had lived the past . . .'

'Yes?' He sounded surprised, or faintly amused. 'Who were they?'

'The servants. All except Johnson and Marie whom I couldn't trace.'

'And what were you hoping for?'

'Reality. A part of reality, at any rate. I'd forgotten that the past is a collective experience.'

He didn't say anything, and I continued: 'I recognized the past all right through their eyes, it was part of me – but I still couldn't understand my part in it. I packed the interviews away and wrote other books.'

'Perhaps it stirred up memories you found painful.'

'Painful? No, I don't think that was it. I couldn't reach the fundamental understanding which would give meaning to it.' As I said it, an abyss opened in front of me. Meaning! What meaning? Perhaps there was none. 'It must have meaning otherwise there's no point,' I added. 'I navigate on those flatlands like a ship on a fog-bound sea . . .'

The simile went unappreciated; instead, rather drily, he commented that I seemed to be coping and was probably coming out of my depression. He would understand if I didn't want to pursue the matter. On the other hand . . .

I thanked him and said I wished to continue.

'In that case, I'm afraid we can't make a start until after the summer break, in September.'

'Oh! . . . All right.'

He got up. 'September 3, if that is convenient.'

'Yes . . .' We shook hands and, as I shut the double doors behind me, I realized there was little enough time to review the evidence I had gathered ten years ago.

2

They

Hic Rhodus, hic salta

The phrase, *Here is Rhodes, leap here*, stares in dusty optimism from the pages of the notebook which, with the yellowing folders, I have retrieved from the attic. It was written, I remember, in tribute to André Gorz whose *The Traitor*, beginning with the phrase, had started me on this trail; a trail which, having led to this particular edge, now beckoned me to leap: *Hic Rhodus . . .*

It was cold, I don't need the notebook to remind me, a cold November afternoon. Across the low-lying fields of plough and seared grass, from which a chill autumn mist was rising, the Manor stood out like a white shadow against the firs on Amnersfield hill. As elusive as an image on the edge of a dream, you thought, hesitating in the unfamiliar gateway. There was nothing else to fix the eyes on. Then, sensed rather than seen, the humped-back bridge spanning the river between the flatlands of Amnersfield and the town emerged through the mist. You walked towards the door and rang Ilse's bell.

The chimes sounded distantly behind the glass door. It was thirty years since you had seen her; the date of that terrible parting remained engraved in the memory: September 1, 1939, two days before the outbreak of war. Your father was in uniform, waiting to go, but he insisted that Ilse leave first to catch the last German liner to call at Southampton; and you had never seen her again. Or even known of her return to England until a few months before when her postcard had arrived out of the blue and you'd put it aside, unthinkingly. It was some time before the realization that chance might be offering a new approach began to sink in. Her reply to your letter, unexpectedly volunteering that Mr and Mrs Carvell, Doris and, she believed, Bert, were still living in the neighbourhood, came as a further stimulus: through *them*, I recall you thinking, you might at last find a way forward – a perspective in which each stood equally witness to a past you had in your different ways shared...

A white-haired woman in an elegant red dress opened the door. Her face was still youthful, but it was only the deep brown eyes that were instantly recognizable. She held out her hand in a formal gesture of greeting as for a moment you both, I suppose, adjusted reality to old images. Her eyes were a little tense, betraying an understandable hesitation, and you were glad to step inside the door. With a slight shrug she took the bottle of wine you offered and led the way into a kitchen of cream walls and white wood where on a table china and silver were laid. While she went to dispose of the bottle you looked round: everything was neat, immaculately clean, as though bathed in sunlight, and it stirred memories of childhood security and well-being.

Ilse returned and stirred a sauce simmering on the stove. 'I hope you like sour cream, your mother always did. And lemon and sugar salad dressing—we always used to have it at the Manor...' Low, accented still, her words were less of an incantation than a deliberate continuation of the past, and it opened avenues back.

Over lunch you chatted casually of the years since the Manor. She had returned to England in the post-war years with a British army officer's family and later had become a nurse in the local hospital; in a couple of years she would retire. A few months before she had seen one of your books in a library, had rung the publishers and been given the address. She had heard of your mother's death, from the Carvells she thought, but of your father, Alexander, she had had no news and you told her the little there was to tell. Getting old was very painful, she agreed, especially now that his third wife had died and he was alone. You turned the conversation away to enquire whether she saw the Carvells often; yes, she said, they remained good friends. She had met Doris on the bus going to Amnersfield once and Doris had mentioned that Bert lived nearby. But Ilse hadn't seen him, which was hardly a surprise. Of the rest she had heard nothing since the war.

After lunch she took the coffee tray into the living room. Through the large window at the end you saw the Manor House glimmering against the horizon of trees. Smiling, you said, That's one thing I didn't expect. You seem to have come full circle...

Oh, I love the countryside, you know, I always have. She sat down in a straight-backed chair. That was my great joy when we were at the Manor. Every evening I would walk over the fields . . .

Ah yes, you said. The moment had come and you reached into the briefcase. Would she mind if you recorded this . . . She nodded, busying herself with the coffee pot and paid no attention as you plugged in the recorder. At that moment, I'm sure, you had no definite idea of what you were going to ask, other than that you should start with memories of her working life at the Manor. You set the machine going and said, For you perhaps it was a place of fields. For me it was a house surrounded by walls . . .

Tape 1, November 15, Start: Surrounded by walls . . .

Walls, Ronnie? Oh no, it was a nice open place. A large garden with lawns, trees and shrubs. I was a little surprised that your parents didn't have flower beds planted, that they didn't do more to make the house attractive. But they were too taken up with other things. I was pleased that the nurseries were in the old Manor, I liked the low ceilings and beams, although some of the rooms were a little dark. Oliver Cromwell stayed there, didn't he? But the front – oh! It had just been stuck on. The rooms were big, without character. The dining room was like a barn, the front hall was panelled in black. I remember I was a little disappointed the first time I saw it and wondered why they hadn't bought a house with more charm as their new home in England . . .

—So you were disappointed at having come?

Oh no, not disappointed. You mustn't think I'm being critical. Life there was interesting in so many other ways. Not much had happened in my life and I found it all rather exciting. To begin with, I'd never worked in a house with as large a staff. A butler, groom, Mr Winteringham in the garden with a boy under him, a cook, two housemaids. I was fascinated by it all, although later I saw that many of the other houses had even larger staffs.

—Can you tell me about the staff at the Manor?

Well, Johnson was the butler, you remember. He was small, not at all manly and he made me feel a little bit – what is the word? – creepy, yes. I know I wouldn't have had him in the house. But he did his job well, waited at table and polished the silver very nicely and looked after your father's clothes. He used to clean his scarlet hunting coat in the pantry which I thought was wrong. Dirty work like that should have been done outside somewhere. But then everything was so different here . . .

Emily, the cook, do you remember her? No? . . . Ilse laughed. Moments before the first dinner party, she saw her squashing potatoes into the serving dish with her hand. Ilse was appalled, remembering the care taken over dinner parties in Hamburg; and she wasn't surprised that before long Emily was asked to leave.

Out in the large garden, Mr Winteringham, a fat jolly man in his late sixties, grew vegetables even more beautiful than she had known in Germany. He was very nice and didn't mind when she picked a tomato or some flowers from the garden. In the evenings she sometimes went over to his cottage by the stables. His wife was very pleasant, a real old English servant who had spent most of her working life in a big house like her husband. She was always telling Ilse how a lady's maid should look after her mistress. It all seemed very old-fashioned.

Before long, Mr Winteringham fell ill and died, of cancer, wasn't it? and his wife and their unfortunate daughter Dolcie stayed on in the cottage. Bert, meanwhile, had come, young and slim with a sludgy sort of walk, not very manly, she thought. A little bit easy, a little bit lazy, not the old type of gardener like Mr Winteringham. He hadn't been there long before he got married. His wife, a fat girl, was a bit untidy. They lived in that run-down cottage at the top of the garden, without running water or sanitation, a really very poor place.

She liked William Carvell, the groom, better than Bert. He was very nice, I mean he came from a nice family, his father had owned a riding stable. He had a funny sort of walk, leaning to one side, and wasn't all that strong. But I thought he did his job well and wasn't someone who would talk behind your back.

—And the maids?

Yes, there was a housemaid and another who helped in the kitchen. She was a sweet girl, I can't remember her name. The two maids slept in one room, the cook had a bedroom of her own and the butler had one of the little rooms in the tower. The maids' rooms were quite inadequate . . . In other houses, she saw later, the staff was organized differently. The first housemaid was brought tea in the morning by the second or third, the nanny had a nursery maid to wait on her, the butler a footman. With a smaller staff at the Manor, more work was expected of the servants on occasion. Even she sometimes felt she was over-worked and could do with a nursery maid; but then she'd tell herself that she was just getting ideas from the other nannies.

What had she been paid, you asked.

About £5 or £6 a month and her fare home on holiday once a year. I was happy with that, although I provided my own uniforms. The rest of the staff had theirs provided... In the house she wore only white, but for going out she put on her nurse's light-blue uniform with white collar and cuffs and a large white apron topped with a white cap. For travelling she added a dark blue veil. It made her look rather like a modern nun, she thought. Other nannies wore grey suits and blouses. After a time, Ilse wanted to abandon her uniform for something less formal, but your mother asked her to go on wearing it.

—Did it make you feel different to other nannies?

Well, I have to say that the nanny's position at the Manor wasn't as clearly defined as in other houses. Emily thought I had no right in the kitchen, Johnson resented having to serve me when we ate in the dining room. But it wasn't serious. I accepted things as they were, that's my way of being. Fatalistic – is that what you call it?

Perhaps, you suggested, the nanny's position between masters and servants had seemed ambiguous to her.

Yes... Although I wasn't treated like one, I felt myself to be more or less a servant. Inferior, I don't know why. Perhaps it had to do with my past, with the fact that I had to go out to work because my mother had lost all her money after the first World War or because I came from a broken home. I felt I shouldn't express opinions, that I had to hide my private life, be industrious, loyal and characterless. I was conscious of it but I didn't suffer. I liked living in nice surroundings and I hated the idea of having to find another position or return to work in an institution. And then, living in the nursery was a bit like being in a world of my own...

A world between worlds, no doubt.

Oh, it was two worlds living under one roof. The masters spoke differently, they had the money to do what they wanted, they were born to their positions and accepted life as it was. It was a very closed world, the Manor

House, a world to itself. All rather feudal, I thought, though Prussia was no doubt worse. The servants gave loyalty and devotion to their master and mistress because that was what was due from them. The young girls seemed quite happy in service without any cultural or even love life. A kitchen maid's ambition was to become second maid or something like that. Each servant was employed for specific tasks and only those. So Emily wouldn't answer the phone even when it went on ringing right outside the kitchen door. That was the butler's job . . .

Ilse laughed. You see, she went on, the masters respected their servants as people who mustn't be asked to do more than they had been employed to do. It was never a matter of getting as much out of them as possible. The masters wanted it known that they occupied a different social level, but then they made it their responsibility to look after their servants, to help them if they were in difficulty. There was far greater consideration for servants here than in Germany.

—What did you make of that?

I liked it, it was the nice side of the English employer. It was all so interesting to me. I had never been in high society before. I mean, here were people who could do whatever they liked, who didn't need to work, who could live to ride and hunt and shoot, play tennis, bridge, entertain one another. I remember once I heard them all shrieking with laughter and I thought, My goodness, they're spending the afternoon playing *Monopoly*! How strange that they don't go to the theatre and opera more! But no, their talk was of horses, their life was taken up with sport . . .

Again she laughed. Have some more coffee. Over the sound of cups being filled she explained that before leaving Hamburg she had made a point of going to every opera, even *The Ring*, because she couldn't leave for England without being familiar with every German composer. At the Manor there wasn't much music, and she missed it. Whenever she went to the Winteringham's or to her English teacher, the wireless seemed invariably to be tuned to Gracie Fields, the popular Lancashire singer, whom Ilse came to think of as the epitome of English culture.

At home in Germany she was used, too, to lively discussions; but again here there was little of that. In the evening, when your mother and father came back from hunting, she would hear them talking about horses from the moment they entered the house. Over dinner, Johnson would tell her, they talked only about which ditch or hedge they had jumped and, after dinner, from the nursery she could hear them still discussing how he had had to ride this way and she that.

—You accepted all this as normal . . .

Yes, I wasn't critical at all. I was fascinated by the different life style. Later I came to think that the life was a bit flat but at the time I enjoyed it. Every evening I went for a walk over the fields. Things were much more peaceful then, the world turned slower. I loved living in the countryside, as I've said, I'm a bit of a romantic, I think. So yes, I accepted everything as it was . . .

A cold, sunny December afternoon. The humped-back bridge twists over the river and canal, dangerously narrow still, and you hear the squeal of brakes as an on-coming car appears over the brow. Sitting on your mother's lap, you see her hands tense on the steering wheel. Then the bang, quite light in reality, but sufficient to jerk your hand with the pencil upwards. Blood spurts into your mouth. Your mother gasps: the pencil has pierced your lip. The other driver clambers out of his car; when he sees where you're sitting he says something sharp to Janey who can find no reply, and you know, once again, that you are guilty . . .

It was raining then; today there is a rime on the hedgerows and stark black trees. It made little difference, you saw. Come sun or rain everything in this river valley was evasive. The flatlands raised hopes of wide views which were instantly deceived by a straggly row of trees, a slight rise, an isolated labourer's cottage. A sense of unease came over you: there was nothing here to please the eye, not even a small immaculate view, before the spiky barrier of firs on Amnersfield hill cut off the horizon.

You got back in the car, fearing that you'd never be reconciled to this transient no-man's-land which you carried inescapably everywhere and constantly fled. With only a glance you drove past the Manor, past old Charlie Tine's crumbling garage which was no longer there; past the two pubs facing each other and Harvey Jones's workshop where two smart new houses stood; past the triangular recreation ground opposite the Manor's end field, and up to the redbrick 1930s bungalow, the first of a row of four, where the Carvells had always lived.

It was cold, drizzling, fields and trees always shrouded in mist or creeping afternoon fog when you went out with him. The cold numbed your feet and hands and, standing by the yellow door, congealed you anew. Were there never days when the air was bright and the countryside clear, when you could see and feel without this icy grip in your bowels? Days of pleasure next to this man, his narrow countryman's face coloured by wind and rain, unchanged, instantly recognizable, the bridge of his nose curiously flattened on one side, the thinning silver hair cut short and brushed close to the head . . . Good heavens! Ilse telephoned to say—How many years? Thirty, is it really? How time goes! . . . Yes, there must have been . . .

Come in, come in . . . The wall-papered living room on the left, chintz covers on the three-piece suite, coal fire burning in the grate, the kitchen where Mrs Carvell had brusquely vanished – fearsome Mrs Carvell who never had a first name – to re-emerge with a tray of sandwiches piled high, home-made cake and strong tea. Well, fancy this! William, turn that thing off! He likes to watch the racing. Come on now, these are specially made . . .

Everything was familiar and yet there was no memory of it. Ilse said you'd been to see her. She's mellowed a bit with the years, hasn't she? Very fond of her we are, she still comes out to visit. William, do turn that thing off . . .

Wistfully, Carvell obeyed, missing the end of the four o'clock race. No, no, don't worry, I just watch it for something to do . . . Horses were still his passion, he followed the hunt when he could, but on foot now. Lady Melbray had been out the other day, he'd seen Sir Geoffrey Huntley a fortnight before, they were about the only ones left whom you might have known . . .

Have you been back to the Manor, then? Mrs Carvell asked. No? Well, it's been divided up, you know. There's a doctor in the old part and a former British embassy counsellor in Japan has the front. The stables and Bert's cottage have been converted. I don't know the people who live in them. There aren't many of the old houses left the way you used to know them.

No, it's a shame, Carvell put in. You don't get the same class of people out hunting any more. The war changed all that, you know.

Yes, it changed a lot – and for the better I always thought, you said. What have you been doing these past years?

Carvell sipped his tea. I never went back to being a groom. I got a job at the Ordnance factory down the road from the Manor. Do you remember it being built on Craigie's land before the war?

Yes . . . Irish labourers and mud on the road in front of the Manor's gates; and a word that stuck threateningly in the memory: war. There was going to be a war, Bert said, and they needed weapons, TNT, that's what the factory was for. It was only three large fields away, you heard the test explosions thump out each afternoon, but you never saw the factory . . . It was underground, wasn't it?

Oh no, not in those days, Carvell replied.

Really? I always believed it was . . . Then the flatlands swallowed everything, even deceived the dark grey German bomber which broke through the cloud one wartime afternoon . . .

Now a lot of it is, though. It's gone atomic, you see. It's where our nuclear weapons are assembled. That's secret, I shouldn't say it.

Nuclear! Really! Well, I suppose with Aldermaston not that far away . . . You know, I always associate Aldermaston with red deer. They fascinated me as a child in the park where the Atomic Weapons place now is. It's about those years before the war that I wanted to talk to you.

Of course, he replied, Ilse had said something about it. If he could be of any help he'd be glad. He found an electric socket close by to plug in the recorder and re-arranged his chair by the fire to accommodate it on the table next to him. Where do you want to start? At the beginning? All right, let's see . . .

I was taken on a good month or more before the Manor was ready to move into and I took the horses across. Goodalls were still redecorating, I remember. It was an attractive house, I thought, not too large but large enough and well situated in the village. There were other, bigger houses in the vicinity but the Manor House always carries prestige. The only thing I would have planned differently was the stables. They were rather enclosed and had been designed for harness horses, not hunters . . .

Only two hunters had been brought over from Germany, but soon they bought three more. At the time, Carvell recalled, a groom thought he was hard done by if he did two horses and a child's pony on his own. Before long he found himself doing twice that number. But Captain and Mrs Fraser had told him when he took over that the horses were in his complete charge and he found his reward in that; the horses were in a way, he felt, his. He loved animals, enjoyed the work. Moreover, he was about to get married at thirty-one and glad to be in a regular job. But it meant very long hours—

You must realize that William is — I mustn't say stupid — but he doesn't stand up for himself. He was always too loyal . . .

—Can we come back to that later, Mrs Carvell? It makes things difficult on the tape if two people talk at once.

She nodded, retreating behind the regular beat of her knitting needles (affectionately noted in the transcript by a now anonymous typist) into a barely containable silence.

Yes, well, that's what she has always said, Carvell laughed. Why didn't I take my bed down to the stables? . . . It was like that, he'd start work at 6 a.m. on an ordinary day, watering, feeding and mucking out. At 7.45 he had to drive the captain to the station to catch the London train, back again to exercise a couple of the horses for half an hour before breakfast, then out again with those that hadn't hunted the previous day for a good hour's exercise. By the time they'd been cleaned and put away comfortable it was half past twelve and time to feed again. An hour's lunch and he'd be back in the harness room, cleaning the saddles, head pieces, steel bits, bridles and hunting kit that had been used the day before. Half the battle was to keep the leather nice and supple so that the horses didn't suffer from bad backs. Yellow soap and glycerine was what we used in those days. With a bit of luck, if he didn't have to chauffeur during the afternoon, he might be finished by six.

On hunting days he started even earlier, having the horses feeding on oats, bran and chaff by 6 a.m. The horses that were hunting would get a good grooming before setting out. He might have to hack ten or twelve miles to the meet and that meant leaving the yard by quarter past nine. Before then he had to wash, shave and change into his groom's brown suit, boots and leggings and bowler hat. Nine times out of ten he'd wear a mackintosh over the coat to keep it clean. By rights, he should have had a new coat every year but they asked him to make do with his for two years.

He set off on the captain's horse, leading Mrs Fraser's which had a side-saddle. They'd come on by car to the meet at 11 and he'd drive the car back. Most days the captain had a second horse which Carvell would saddle up as soon as he got back and, after a quick bite, ride out to pick up the hounds. He knew every inch of the country, he'd been hunting since he was a boy; his father had a jobmaster's business – a livery yard it would be called now – buying and selling and letting out hunters. Even if he couldn't find the hunt the horse soon would; he'd cock his ears and Carvell would know which way to go. They'd change horses anywhere between one and half past, reckoning two hours of hunting for each horse.

Thursday was the main day because the hunt was in the best part of the country, the vale. The Frasers liked the big fields with plenty of galloping and jumping, weren't happy unless they'd jumped twenty fences a day. They weren't like the people who went hunting because it was etiquette and were content with a few hours' hacking in the woodlands, no, they wanted to have a real go and were always in the first half dozen, up with the hounds.

What had happened, you asked, after he had taken the fresh horse out.

I'd bring the first one home and clean him. Then, depending on how far away the hunt ended, I'd take the car out for them or they'd hack home. If I took the car they'd drive back on their own and I'd bring the horses home. It could be half past six before I got back in the dark – we didn't bother about lights in those days . . .

In the stables he'd loosen the horses' girths and get them to pass water. A horse should never have his gruel of linseed before urinating. Then one of the parlour maids brought him a pot of tea, a boiled egg, bread and butter before he got down to the real work. Bridles and saddles off, loose rugs on, the horses eating a nice warm bran mash after the gruel, and he rubbing them down with plenty of straw to take the dirt off. As soon as the horses' ears felt dry their bodies were dry. A wet horse meant coughs, cracked heels or mud fever. The secret was warmth – cotton wool and bandages round all four legs – and dryness. A feed of oats, bran and chaff – more oats than bran – and he went into the saddle room.

It would be eight o'clock easily by then. He sponged all the saddles and bridles and cleaned what he could and it was gone nine before he went quietly back into the stables. If a horse was standing, he felt his ears and ran his hand over the loins to make sure the body was nice and dry. Try him with one more drink of lukewarm water, a bit more hay in the nets and shut them up for the night. On hunting days he very seldom left before a quarter to ten.

—Very long hours. Did you never protest?

No. I daresay I was a bit soft but I was glad to have a secure job. It was the Manor House and I thought it was a job for life which it might have been but for the war. I didn't care what happened outside the stables to be quite honest. I was happy with the horses, they were my responsibility. I decided which horses they would ride, they left all that to me, not like Lady Melbray, say, who would tell her groom what he had to do. I had a certain power, you see. It was hard work, there were no weekends off. If the work didn't get done on Saturday then it had to be done on Sunday ready for hunting the next day. But all the same I was doing a job I enjoyed . . .

—What did you get paid?

Thirty five shillings a week at the start, with an extra five shillings when I got married. We turned down the offer of the cottage where Bert used to live and then I got another five shillings to help pay the rent here which was fourteen shillings a week. Most grooms had a cottage, lighting and firing and thirty shillings a week. I was left with thirty-one shillings after paying the rent but I had neither coal nor light. I knew I was underpaid. The gardener got all his vegetables, lighting and firing . . .

—Have you any idea how much it cost to keep a horse in those days?

To feed and shoe, even then, without veterinary bills, you wouldn't do it for under fifty shillings, perhaps £3 a horse a week.

—You mean, it cost more to keep a horse than it did you?

Well, yes, if you put it like that . . .

There was a silence; in the shadow by the fire Mrs Carvell's knitting needles clicked impatiently. When she spoke it was with anger in her voice:

William put up with all sorts of indignities at the Manor. He worked for a paltry sum from sunrise to sunset and longer because he was too loyal. He's such a noble type, he deserved much better – double the wage at least – and a lad to help him. But then, it was his fault too, he could have left. He wouldn't. Having been left high and dry at thirty-odd when his father's livery yard failed he was glad to accept anything. He was stupid, I felt, he wouldn't stick up for himself . . .

Her bitterness of thirty years erupted without indulgence. Carvell said nothing, having heard it many times, no doubt. A morbid satisfaction at her outspokenness, a sense of touching a nerve of truth, led you on: what indignities was she thinking of?

All this, Yes, Madam, No, Madam stuff. I may be a little bolshevik about this but I wasn't used to all the bowing and scraping. It irritated me. And then he'd be up at half-past five and I might not see him again for hours and hours . . .

But it wasn't only the hours, it was the hurt she felt for him when he was hurt. The Frasers never did any of those personal little things that, lacking money, would have meant a lot to them, like offering to run them down to the seaside for their week's holiday. The groom at the Old Rectory was much better treated, the Winchesters thought the world of him. He got better money and they always made sure that if he needed anything for his children he got it. It all made Mrs Carvell feel that her husband was being used. In private service you were always thought to earn less than in an ordinary job with a salary because of the little things you got in lieu – the things that the gentry did at the time. But we never got anything in lieu, that was the trouble . . .

—How do you explain all this?

I think I was to blame, perhaps . . .

—Why?

Well, I wouldn't go to work in the house if they needed help like Mrs Winteringham or Bert's wife. I had my profession as a nurse and I felt they couldn't ask me to work as an ordinary servant. I'd never done it and I didn't want to. As a nurse I'd met all kinds of people who were monied and high in the world, especially when I worked in a private clinic in London. The Duke of Gloucester and other nobility were patients and they always made me feel on a level with them though I was only a girl of twenty-two. I'd looked after far better types of people, and here was William being treated far worse down at the Manor. That was my biggest resentment. He deserved much better . . .

Thirty years ago, heathland stretched away on either side of the road beyond the fir-covered hill: heather and gorse, bracken and sandy paths which led to dark pools where the horses would stop to drink. The shrouded fields and hedges vanished below the hill, behind the tall firs where rooks cawed angrily from inaccessible nests; the road ran straight, after its sharp ascent, across the common – Amnersfield Common, a short line of working-class houses, Victorian village school, Jubilee Hall – to the *Rising Sun* where the hunt sometimes met on the heathland's entangled openness. A thorny green sea hiding treacherous drops where, Carvell warned, a horse could easily break a leg, it was always an uncertain, alien place.

And perhaps of what remains may still be so. But little remains. A century and more ago the London railway opened the Amnersfield countryside to a bourgeoisie in search of a country gentleman's station in life. Their vast and numerous mansions, little changed fifty years later, were the gloomy mausoleums of your childhood. Today, as Mrs Carvell said, most have been converted to other ends: old people's homes, boarding schools for Inner London councils, Borstals . . . The motorway, cutting a swathe across the flatlands on the far side of the river, has covered the countryside with London's overflow: nuclear weaponry and ranch-house estates for city commuters.

It was not to one of these but to an old labourer's cottage, close by the *Rising Sun*, that Mrs Carvell directed you. A small, grey-haired woman opened the door. You looked at each other blankly for a moment. Mrs Jones? . . . Yes . . . Who used to work at the Manor? I don't suppose you recognize me . . . No, I can't say – well, I never! As soon as I saw you I knew there was something. You're the splitting image of your mum . . .

Yes? . . . In the small, sparsely furnished front room, where a paraffin stove gave off a familiar sweetish smell and little warmth, Eileen repeated, Yes, no mistaking. I heard you'd gone abroad, don't know who told me . . . Her attention divided between pulling up a chair and apologizing for the state of the room, she said she had just come in from work. Since her divorce a few years ago, life hadn't been easy. She'd had to go out cleaning again which was a bit of a come down. But she couldn't complain, she was happy to have her own life, her own home. One couldn't ask for more, could one?

She went out to make fresh tea and returned laughing. At the Manor one summer, she recalled, there had been a big tennis party and tea on the lawn. It was her Sunday on and she had brought out the silver teapot and when Mrs Fraser poured only water came out. A great cheer went up from the guests and ever after Eileen had been teased when she made tea . . .

Can you tell me what your life at the Manor was like?

The work and that, you mean?

Yes, to begin with, you said, turning on the recorder.

Well, I was housemaid, house parlour-maid actually, since there was no one over me. We used to get up at six and work until eight without anything to eat, I remember that well enough. First I'd do the fireplaces and tidy up the drawing room and then the smoking room. It was the fireplace that took the most time. You had to black the hearth and polish it, then clean the stone around it with red powder. I'd put the coal-scuttles out and Bert would fill them. All this took until breakfast. I was as hungry as a horse by then. I was only seventeen. And all we got for breakfast was a streaky rasher of bacon, half a piece of fried bread and a cup of tea. They were a bit mean with the food where the staff was concerned . . .

—Was that true of other houses, do you know?

I couldn't rightly say. I don't think it was intentional at the Manor, just that people in that position had their own social life and what happened out in the kitchen didn't bother them unless complaints got through.

—Did you never complain?

No. Not that it's ever bothered me to ask for what I want. I've never thought of myself as being very much lower than other people. But I was young then and I thought that was my lot . . . After the dining-room breakfast, she and Doris used to ask the cook if there were any bits; the maids did that in all the houses. If they were lucky they might get a piece of fried bread left over from the dining room where they had bacon and eggs, scrambled eggs, kedgeree, which the captain was fond of, sausages, kidneys, all the usual sort of things. The staff got a special Sunday breakfast of sausage and egg.

After breakfast, she began cleaning upstairs; the master bedroom and the dressing room next to it were her first task. The Manor was a big rambling place which used to get very dirty because it was so old. It took all morning to get through the cleaning. After lunch, there was the washing-up and then she was free for an hour until tea. During that period she would sew for Mrs Fraser while Doris, with whom she shared a bedroom, sewed for the nursery.

In her coffee-coloured afternoon uniform, with its lace-backed cuffs and collar, a little apron and coffee-coloured lace cap which Mrs Fraser had had specially made for her, Eileen felt she looked quite smart. She's serve tea in the drawing room or smoking room, just a light tea of sandwiches, muffins or scones and then, if there was a dinner party that evening, she'd set the dining-room table. It was this that she loved most of all, the frequent dinner parties.

The table always looked so lovely, the silver and the candles and the glass, and then the ladies coming in their evening dresses. She'd stand in the hall with Johnson and he would take the men's coats and she the ladies' and hang them in the cloakroom by the front door. Many of the guests she would know and she'd say, Good evening, Lady Melbray . . . Good evening, Eileen, it's very cold out tonight . . . Then the guests went into the drawing room for sherry and cocktails which Johnson served until he announced dinner. She would be waiting in the dining room and together they would show the guests to their places. The captain always sat at the end of the table by the door opposite Mrs Fraser at the far end.

Eileen would bring in the first course, paté or vol-au-vent it might be, which would be followed by fish, meat, savoury, sweet, cheese and biscuits and then fruit. They used to eat well, you know, six or seven courses always, and all the different wines which Johnson served. He needed a steady hand for that, but he liked to finish the dregs in the cocktail shaker and he was usually a bit tiddly. Sometimes I held him up so that they wouldn't see or walked round just behind him to make sure he didn't fall over. He was a capable butler really, and didn't drink on duty except at dinner parties, but it used to worry me that he might not make it. Afterwards, the cook and I would drag him to his bedroom and dump him on the bed. He never knew how he got there.

In the dining room there was lots of laughter and chatter. It was always a jolly atmosphere. Eileen remained throughout, but she never took much notice of the conversation because she was brought up not to be nosy. I can shut my ears off if I don't want to hear something, I've got that habit . . .

—Did you feel that because you were a servant you didn't exist for them, that they could safely ignore you?

No, I don't think so, because as you walked round the table serving them they'd smile and say, Hello, how are you? They got to know us. We were never looked down on, weren't treated like skivvies. We were part of the family, more or less, you see . . .

As soon as the sweet course was finished the ladies withdrew and Johnson took the gentlemen in their coffee and port. It wasn't long before loud laughter was heard from the dining room. My God, won't they ever go, I used to think out in the pantry doing the washing-up. And sometimes they stayed so long that Mrs Fraser would call, Come along, Alexander, we're waiting to play bridge...By that time poor old Johnson wasn't awake enough to take the drinks through to the drawing room and I'd slip in with the tray and out again before they had time to notice. On those nights I got to bed very late – we were never in bed before ten anyway and up again at six. But I was young and it didn't seem to harm me.

—You give the impression of enjoying the work...

Yes, I did. People wouldn't want to do it today, but things were different then. There wasn't a lot of work round Amnersfield way and you were lucky to have a job. To my way of thinking, in private service you were superior to factory people, say. In service you were in a different world, a world of your own. You learned to speak different because you were with people who spoke well. Of course, there were long hours. We only had a half day and alternate Sunday mornings and afternoons off. Even then we had to be in by 10 p.m. But I was my own boss and I liked that. Everybody mucked in and helped. It was much more like a big family then...

A happy family, moreover. Emily was replaced by an Austrian cook, Marie, who wasn't much older than Eileen and Doris. Nanny and Johnson were a bit older, but not too much. Eileen felt at home with the staff. In fact, I felt a part of the house, it was a little community and we were all quite happy. We were never made to feel we had to hurry in and out so as not to be seen...

The only person she didn't get on with at times was nanny. Once, when the vacuum cleaner was out of order, nanny wanted the stairs to the night nursery cleaned. She kept on and on about those stairs – she was very military-like, you know – until I thought, Right if you want the stairs swept I'll sweep them. And I swept the stairs as hard as I could, taking all the dust to the top. Then I got a broom and, nasty little thing that I was, swept everything into nanny's bedroom. There you are, I said, you've had your stairs brushed, now you can clear it up...She glared at me but didn't say anything. I meant to show her that nobody's ever sat on me, even if I have to work for my living...

In their fading folders the transcripts continue for three more interviews. The diary reveals several visits a week to Amnersfield at this period. On December 11, the day after visiting Eileen and the Carvells, you set out again, turning this time, however, into the town to find, with difficulty, the cul-de-sac of Victorian workers' cottages which were as little part of any recognizable past as Ilse's new home on the outskirts.

Opening the wooden gate, crossing the path to the low door, you waited hesitantly for an answer to your knock. Then Bert was standing there and his, Well, look who we've got here, swept you across the threshold into a past of inadmissable pleasures, the familiarly unfamiliar clutter of a child-hood treasure trove. Mother, he called, and from the scullery at the back came a familiar voice. Sit down then if you can find a bit of room . . . He gestured sharply at one of two large armchairs which, with a sofa, a yellow plastic table, a chest holding a TV, another larger chest beside the door and two buckets of firewood took up most of the small room's floor space.

You sank into the chair, feeling the warmth of the fire behind a familiar crested guard above which, on the mantlepiece, were displayed brightly polished brass cartridges, ashtrays, a peevish looking frog, bottle openers, rag dolls, old postcards and one of the two large clocks in the room. A budgie sat on its perch in a cage. Mrs Sells came in, her bulk swimming with ease of long habit through the obstructions and constrictions. Well, I never! I don't know if I'd of recognized you, you didn't use to wear glasses, did you? . . . Look at that mother, Bert put in, he's still got man-ners, standing up. Brought up proper, he was. He laughed . . . Don't take any notice of him, she said, he hasn't changed . . . Bert dropped his thin, rakish body into the other armchair. You don't want to put on no airs for the missus. Now, what's blown you in?

They had received your letter, hadn't they? Yes, well, as you had tried to explain, it would be a sort of record, a bit of history, it was important to know what the past had been like. On one side of the fireplace you caught sight of the glass-fronted display case that Ron Jones's father made to show off not the crockery it now held but your Me 109, Blenheim Mk IV, the awkward bird-winged Lysander, a black Beaufighter . . . and smelt again the sweet dealwood dust as the treadle fretsaw cut out the shape of the war-time model planes . . . Well, I don't know, you heard Bert say, can't see the point of it myself . . . The heavy Berkshire accent which, but for an undertone of cockney, might be taken for west country, hadn't changed; but his eyes had lost their sharp look.

Those times, the memory of those times mustn't be lost, you insisted. On top of the cabinet was the old radio set with the green eye that grew large and small as Lord Haw-Haw's voice grew louder or fainter, as *ITMA* and *Monday Night at Eight* came over the air . . . I'll tell you the best thing about those times and that is that they're dead and gone for ever. Never come back, thank God. The workers won't have it today. The class, whatever you want to call them, they're even lower now than us... He chortled, watching out of the corner of his eye to see your reaction.

Wait a minute, you said. You didn't want him to start yet and bent down to open the briefcase at your feet.

Oh-ho! he exclaimed. What you got there? A tape-recorder? Look at that then, mother... Mrs Sells smiled without replying. Who's going to hear this? No one but you? You've got to be careful, you never know.

You put the small cassette on the table beside him. It won't bite, talk a bit. Have you ever heard your voice?

It's not the bite I'm worried about, it's the bark. Is that thing on? Come on, mother, say a word...

Tape Starts: *Come on, mother, say a word*... Faithfully transcribed, evidence presumably of your failure to erase them, the words stand meaninglessly at the head of the page. Small matter. Two hundred dusty pages of Bert, preserved in red folders, survive. In the last a series of 8x5 inch cards, each under a different heading, forms an index of his experiences scattered through the transcripts. For once your need for order, clarity, served a useful purpose.

Let's see, it's not until the second interview that he says:

It was the time of the slump, you see, and there were dozens out of work. The Labour Exchange sent a card out to several chaps saying there was this gardener's job going at the Manor House. I hadn't had a regular job for two years, just odds and ends here and there. I was never stumped right out, but it was sort of tough. Everybody was in the same boat, so I was glad when they said I was to go for an interview. That was June, 1934.

The Manor was a nice big place, a good kitchen garden and the fields all grass, an ordinary gentleman's estate. I was called into the drawing room, lovely it was, and Mrs Fraser engaged me on the spot to start the following Monday. I was to take over until old Winteringham recovered from his operation. Five shillings a day and half a crown for Saturday, 27/6d a week. In clover again, you see.

—In clover on 27/6d a week?

Of course. It was regular money coming in, something to look forward

to. And then Winteringham got worse from the cancer of the throat, took
to his bed and popped off. That was how I came to stay.

—How big was the garden in fact?

About an acre of kitchen garden and the same again, if not more, of
lawns, shrubbery and trees. It was too much for one man but probably not
enough for two full-time . . . Little had been done when he started and he
had a job to catch up. Mrs Fraser wanted a lot of vegetables most people
hardly knew. Kohlrabi, salsify, corn on the cob, celeriac, Jerusalem arti-
chokes, red cabbage, celery. Each morning he went to the kitchen for
orders. Gardening was the most unthankful job there was, you never got
any praise, only blame. If you had some nice early peas, say, and you knew
you'd got them before anybody else, they wouldn't come out and say, We
enjoyed those peas . . . But if they went out somewhere and had peas
they'd want to know why you hadn't got them. Probably you'd lost the
first sowing or you'd had a packet of dead seeds. You couldn't rely on the
seeds, there was every pest and disease and none of the fungicides and
sprays like now . . .

—Flowers?

Pot plants for the house, chrysanths, cineraria, primulas, geraniums.
There was no what I'd call nice flower beds. Two or three hundred salvia
bedded out, like where I am now, or a bed with nothing but mixed asters. It
makes a smashing show.

Had he suggested anything like that, you enquired.

No, I mean, she might have said, Well, it suits me all right as it is, what
are you worrying about? You got the impression you might be speaking
out of turn. It seemed they weren't interested, just wanted plenty of vegetables, the hedges clipped, the lawn kept nice. Now there was a job. We
had a donkey for that, Heather she was called, that pulled a heavy, old-
fashioned mower. She had leather shoes to keep her hooves from marking
the grass. If she thought she wouldn't go, she wouldn't. And all of a sudden, once she was going, she'd be taken short and I'd shout to the boy,
Look out! and he'd run back and get the box to put under her. That's the
truth.

—You had a boy to help you then?

For about a year, then they sacked him because they couldn't afford the twelve bob a week. Well, it wasn't a question of afford. They never went short of anything, that's what always amused me. But I never asked for another boy – no, that I didn't. Probably they'd have said, If you can't manage on your own we'll get somebody who can. There was ten or fifteen blokes ready to step in if a man got out. And then God knows when you'd get back in. That feeling you mustn't ask for anything. You had to keep out there, even when it was swilling down. You were always under the impression that if you didn't work you wouldn't get paid . . .

Soon he found himself no longer just a gardener but a jack of all trades. Driving, getting wood in, looking after chickens, cutting the hedge round the estate. Nothing had been said at the interview about these extra jobs which started after he got married and his wage was increased by 2/6d a week. He'd be a mass of dirt from garden work when the message came, Bring the car round to the front in half an hour, and he'd rush off home and change into his uniform – breeches and leggings, a blue overcoat and peaked cap in winter, a blue suit and cap in summer – and bring the Vauxhall round. Out they'd come. Afternoon, Madam . . . He'd open the door, shut it behind them and walk round the back of the car. That was something you was always taught, you didn't walk round in front once they were in the car. That was your place, you see, behind. Drive them to wherever it was, back again, go through all the paraphernalia of changing and back to work in the garden. Course, things was getting behind all the time. The weeds were up that high once and the governor came round. What're you doing, he said, a bit of bloody hay-making? . . .

He was very abrupt, the governor, you know, very sarcastic. I mean, we were no more than a heap of dirt in his eyes. Lord of the Manor, he was. He'd walk by in the garden and never speak. Sooner have died than go near a cabbage. Many's the morning he's come out of the front door and I've been wheeling a barrow of coke across the yard to the stoke-hole and he'd just glare at me. Very seldom he'd say, good morning, unless perhaps he'd had a bit of luck. Just glare through those little glasses he wore, his pipe stuck in his mouth. I'd look the other way because I thought if I said anything he might say, I never spoke to you . . . You were only supposed to speak to them if they spoke first. That was the hard and fast rule. You were nothing, you were at their beck and call. But if he stopped and said something, I'd put the barrow down and say, Good morning, sir, and touch my cap.

—Touch your cap?

Course. There was a thick laurel hedge – do you remember? – that closed off the yard. You couldn't lean a ladder against it, to clip it you had to climb up inside. The governor came out of the stables one morning to go hunting and his horse started to prance about. Can't you get out of that bloody hedge, you're frightening my horse, he shouted. Very angry. I could have thrown the clippers at him, but you knew you daren't. You were frightened to say too much. You old sod, I said to myself.

Other times he'd be sweeping leaves in the front drive and the governor came by in the car and drove over the heaps. Bert imagined that he smiled to himself as he did it. But he didn't know, because you mustn't look at them as they went by in the car. And that was another thing, when they had anybody coming, you had to keep out of the way. We've got some friends coming down, we don't want you getting round the front, the governor would say. Very good, sir . . . That's all there was to it. I mean, they didn't want to see scruffs out there when they were going around or playing tennis. All they wanted was a few old serfs to get them vegetables and things.

—What did you feel when he wouldn't even say good morning to you or shouted?

It hurt. But you forgot it, and the next time if he'd speak you'd be happy enough, you wouldn't bear a grudge. It was a recognized sort of thing. Real impolite they were, though. I used to hear them when they were out there banging the ball about on the tennis court. You could always hear the women, they've got them loud, high voices. Real la-di-dah. Now you take the working class, you can't hear them talking six foot away, but the gentry talks so you can hear them a mile off. They don't come straight down to earth with two or three words, either, and they've got no manners because they don't speak to the working class, don't have any conversation with them. A pig can't speak, he's got no conversation, therefore they're more or less the same . . .

Who was your mother? the old man asks. Which one?
Can't you remember? The windscreen wipers rush back
and forth, hissing like repressed laughter. No. He fumbles
again in his pocket, brings out his wallet, looks in it and
returns it to his pocket. I haven't brought any money, old boy.

Can't you remember?

What? He hunches up in his old overcoat as though facing the rain beating against the windscreen, small, defeated. His eyes behind the glasses are watering, his hand wanders again to his pocket and the wallet which has three five-pound notes in it.

It's not a time you remember, is it?

A time? ... He counts the notes. The wash of a passing car hits the windscreen, blotting out the road. The wipers agitatedly clear the glass. He returns the wallet to his pocket, stares straight ahead. I don't know, old man, we never had much ambition for each other, did we?

Sitting on the edge of the chintz settee, Doris looked hesitant as though her words could not match the spotless order of her living room. Everything about it and her, from the ornate plates on the pink wall to the shiny round glasses which framed her face, gave the appearance of being devoted to tidiness. A tidiness reflected in her manner, you thought, as you listened to her explain that she had just turned fifteen when she applied for a job at the Manor; she had heard that they wanted a nurserymaid. When she was small, her grandfather had been a gardener there and she remembered him taking her round once and showing her the greenhouses. Doris was pleased to be taken on; she had had to give up her first job at Halworth House because of housemaid's knee.

And what had she thought of the Manor, you asked.

Her reply was as unexpected as it was rapid:

A hunked old house it was, creepy. That room in the tower next to the butler's was supposed to be haunted. My friend Eileen wouldn't go up there to turn down the butler's bed without me coming too. And on my afternoons off my dad always came down with me because it was scary being next to the churchyard ...

You leant over and switched on the recorder. Relating her fears seemed to have made her less nervous.

– Could we start at the beginning? Can you tell me first what you had to do in your job?

Oh yes. I began at the Manor when your brother, Colin, was just a few months old. I loved children, loved the nursery work, but I was expected to do a lot of other jobs as well. I was as much an extra maid as a nursery-maid . . .

Up at six, she cleaned the hall before getting the nursery breakfast and bringing it to Ilse and the children. Then there were the day and night nurseries to clean, the bathroom. When those were finished she helped out in the kitchen. For mornings she wore a blue uniform with a big white apron; and for afternoons a paler blue dress and a clean apron and cap. She earned thirty shillings a month with board and keep.

The worst for me was being in the kitchen. Marie, the Austrian cook, was very temperamental. Once she threw a knife at the butler's pantry door – really quick-tempered she was, with Johnson especially. Of course, he was very moody, too, and all of a sudden he'd put his foot in it with Marie and the sparks would fly. At other times they'd be chummy. Once they decided that they wouldn't eat with us maids and for about six weeks they ate alone in the kitchen. There wasn't anything Eileen or I could do about it.

—Was there something going on between them?

Well, I was innocent then – they're not so innocent at fifteen nowadays – but, thinking back, I can imagine there was . . . One evening, after she and Eileen had turned down Johnson's bed and were standing by the huge tower window looking out over the stable yard, they were startled by a terrific scream. They bolted back to their room. After a while curiosity got the better of them and they crept downstairs. They were too scared to ask Marie because there'd have been a flow of Austrian and a shouted, Get out of my kitchen . . . so they asked Johnson who had screamed. Nanny, he said, but they never found out what had happened.

—Most of your work must have been with Ilse. How did you find her?

Oh, she was a jolly good worker. She told me from the start what she wanted doing. I was the first nursery maid she'd had. She was very very thorough. She liked all the paintwork washed down once a week and that was quite a job in those days without detergents. I used to think she was a bit too thorough but later, as I got older, I came to see how important it is to be clean and tidy.

—Could you compare her to other nannies at the time whom you knew?

Well, they were English nannies, do you know what I mean? You can't really judge. I mean, I was at the Melbrays as a temporary nursemaid once and there was more – how shall I put it? – more of a family feeling between the nanny and Sir Harold and Lady Melbray. Ilse was in the family but there wasn't the same closeness. It could have been Ilse herself, of course, because she was a bit starchy, like her uniforms. The other nannies were motherly, cuddly, sort of thing, there was an easy, smooth atmosphere around them. Ilse was always bustlely, never relaxed. She had a sort of stiffness about her. And then, you could never get to the bottom of her. Some people's faces you can read but not hers. It was a mask. She had such dark unreadable eyes and they were everywhere, there was nothing she missed . . .

Maybe, Doris thought, she couldn't warm to Ilse because she was a foreigner. You didn't accept foreigners as easily in those days as we do now. I mean, there weren't nearly so many. At that time there was no feeling between the English and the Germans, was there?

Looking out of Ilse's window across the hedge-hatched fields and wet winter ploughs, seeking in silence a memory that floats on the edge of recall: a white-uniformed presence fleetingly glimpsed – was that it? – at the nursery window, back door, kitchen, somewhere . . . watching, as you stand watching Bert, yes, pierced by her irremissible gaze: ever-present Ilse whose eyes, searching out the darkness within, impel you to turn from her: postures of defence . . . walls – walls to erect, walls to protect – and above them the watch-tower guarding your life: all-seeing Ilse whom you hear, through the hypnotic sense of security her voice has once more induced, saying that she led you out to other houses enclosed behind other walls, that was her pleasure . . .

. . . It was like reading a book, I was fascinated to see how they lived. I remember the first time we went to Sir Harold and Lady Melbray's. Nanny Melbray was a huge woman who sat just like a mother hen with her chicks about her. She had a nurserymaid who did the running around. The nursery, which was very large, was at the top of the house and almost a separate unit. The house itself was huge and there was a very large staff. My first shock came when I saw the two children, James and Susan, eating their tea. How terrible, I thought. Look at these children just throwing things on the floor! They didn't behave at all nicely and nanny Melbray didn't tell them how to eat . . .

Lady Melbray never came into the nursery while Ilse was there. She was very much the Lady and never spoke to her. A thin woman, too thin to be graceful, she was a great horsewoman and a bit horsey herself, Ilse thought. Sir Harold was a tubby, jolly type who was Master of the Hunt and a JP or something. Ilse never saw him in the nursery either. It seemed to her that the parents lived for themselves, seeing the children for half an hour or so before they were sent back to the nursery. There wasn't much family feeling in the house.

It was nanny Walker Ilse liked best. She was a great organizer, always keen on going places. She had a very free hand, she had only to say, We must do this or that, for Mrs Walker to agree. Small, dark, friendly, she seemed to Ilse to occupy a superior position in the house compared to other nannies. Perhaps it was due to her personality, perhaps because the Walker household was warm and friendly. Like all the others, Mr Walker didn't have to work; he spent a lot of time out shooting which was what he seemed to enjoy most. Mrs Walker, on the other hand, was a great huntswoman.

At first, Ilse's lack of English meant she had little conversation with the other nannies. But later she discovered that there wasn't an awful lot to talk about with them. Nanny Walker's interests were her children or the children of the other houses. She told Ilse about them. Nothing else. None of the nannies knew about music or the theatre. Ilse used to try to persuade nanny Walker to go to London with her on their day off, something which Ilse did quite often, visiting museums and churches, Hampton Court, the East End, the National Gallery and the Tate on outings which she planned meticulously the evening before with a map of London and the bus and underground timetable in front of her; but there was no getting nanny Walker to leave the house because John would get so upset if she did. He was a lively, adventurous sort of boy, and I thought she spoilt him. As for his sister, Deborah, what didn't nanny Walker have to put up with! She was a terrible child. If I had been looking after her she'd have had a good smack, it would have done her good. But none of the nannies or parents smacked their children. The nannies were there to give the child everything it wanted and needed, not to form its character. That wasn't the nanny's role.

—Wasn't this a very closed world for you?

No, I liked it, mainly because of Nanny Walker. She was always full of ideas, she made life more interesting. I found it a bit boring when we had to stay at home, just playing with the children . . .

—Yes . . . An unwarranted sense of emptiness overcame you suddenly. She wouldn't play, she had work to do. You went into the garden to watch Bert, standing on the path careful not to get dirty, and waited for her white shadow to appear at a window, door, somewhere . . .

—Life outside was more interesting for you, then . . . You must have been involved in an eternal round of children's tea parties, weren't you? What did the nannies do?

Saw that their children had something to eat and ate themselves. We were guests, the food was handed round by the servants, although sometimes the nannies just stood behind their children's chair. When there were games we helped. I was more active than many of the nannies because I felt rather stupid just sitting there. As a rule there was an entertainer or a conjuror. I often wondered whether the children really enjoyed the parties because things were over-organized, it seemed often that they had just enough grace to get through the afternoon. I remember once John and Deborah Walker's grandparents, who were very wealthy and lived in a lovely old house at Brewley, gave a tea-party for over a hundred children. Most of them had chauffeurs and there were all the nannies. When I looked at the table afterwards I suddenly thought, A hundred poor children could have tea just from what's left over. That was the only time I'd made such a comparison. I was much too carried away by events, got too much of a thrill from all the new things that were happening to me to think deeply about these things.

—Still, you must sometimes have thought about the fact that these families could all employ nannies, didn't you?

I found it perfectly natural. That was how things were done in these wealthy families here. I was glad there were people who could employ me, glad to have a job where I was more or less on my own . . .

—Through the other nannies you must have got a view of what they thought about the families they worked for . . .

No, we never discussed them, they were taken for granted. That was one of the nice things about the nannies – there was no gossip . . . Ilse hated gossip; and, although she hadn't thought about it at the time, the nannies would have thought it disloyal to talk about their employers. To be critical wouldn't have entered my head, I don't want you to think that.

—But you have just been very critical . . . The Melbray and Walker children . . .

Oh, those were just my first impressions. Later I got used to it – that was the way those children were brought up, that was how each nanny behaved. I never discussed what I thought with nanny Walker or nanny Melbray.

—Did you always call them nanny Walker, nanny Melbray?

Yes. We all did. It's terrible, isn't it? I didn't know nanny Walker's name until I came back to England after the war and discovered she was called Lily . . .

—The last time you were talking about the gentry, about the way they spoke. What did you think of a situation where one percent of people were rich enough to live the way they wanted and the rest were either out of work or badly paid?

Well, it didn't matter what we thought, we just had to put up with it.

—Yes, but I'm asking what did *you*, Bert, think?

Well, why should it be that they'd got all that bloody money . . .

—Yes? . . .

He shrugged in silence; cautious, defensive, he had postponed the start of the interview for as long as he could.

—Well, what about when you saw the masters going off to hounds, spending their time amusing themselves?

Lucky devils, you thought, galloping about and enjoying themselves, while you've got to slog all day in the garden. And when they come home they throw their horses to the groom and walk off, knowing everything's ready for them, hot baths, food . . .

His eyes looked down towards the corner of his mouth where his upper lip trembled in a familiar moment of anticipation. With hardly a movement of his lips the words came out in a slur:

When the hunt had its meet at the Manor where did all the gentry go? Round the front on the lawn, drinking whisky and that. And where was I? Out in the field with the roughs with a bottle of the cheapest rack beer. If it wasn't drunk quick it had to be thrown away.

He chortled. Same thing when they went out shooting. All the gentry'd be sitting in their cars having their lunch and a nip of whisky while us poor buggers who'd been doing the beating would be under a tree with a sandwich trying to keep out of the rain. At the end – oh yes, they'd give us a rabbit they'd blown to bits. Never a pheasant or partridge, not on your life. Rabbits they wouldn't eat, nor pigeons. They couldn't get their bloody great carving knives round a pigeon's breast, whereas us with a penknife was a different matter. Sometimes the governor would bang on our door and drop a pigeon he'd shot in the fields. Never stop, just bang on the door.

—Didn't he ever stop to talk to you?

No, they didn't mix with us class, they'd walk by you as if you was a heap of muck. They classed you as a worker and that was it. I never really spoke to him all the years I was at the Manor. Except once when he wanted to know why the sewage pump kept getting blocked up. And I said to him one day, all the bloody carrots have come up wrapped in cellophane . . .

—You said what?

No, laughing, the drains kept getting blocked up and half the reason of it was what the governor put down them. And then the things would get round the valves of the pump and they'd stretch and go, *plop-plop*. One day when he was walking round I thought, I'll bloody well out and tell him. I don't like to tell you this, sir, I said, but you know what's blocking them valves up? . . . No, he says . . . Well, come and have a look . . . He just poked his head round the door and said, Ugh! and away he went . . .

You both laughed.

And I'll tell you another thing that used to hurt, he went on. The food. There was more thrown away after one of their parties than we'd have probably for a month. We were scrubbing along on twenty-five bob a week, with a job to get a bit of bread and dripping, something I wouldn't eat now. But you had to then.

—Another sign of their superiority . . .

Oh, they'd do anything to show they're sort of everything and you're nothing, the scum of the earth. Now and again they'd think it was time to give the poor old villagers a treat, a flower show or a fête. Lady so-and-so would be walking round and she'd see a kid. Oh, poor little chap! and she'd open her handbag full of notes and sort through it to find two pennies.

Here you are, my little chap, have a go in the lucky dip . . . Tricks, show off, that's what it was. And the people said, Oh, she's so kind, Lady so-and-so, she gave my boy twopence.

—The gentry ran the county, didn't they? What did a gentleman mean to you – in class terms, I mean?

It's only money after all, isn't it? They're all men and women, only they've got money, they try to talk posher than the average bloke and they won't mix with the poor class.

—Didn't you ever think things could be changed?

Not at all. Not at all, because we were brought up, all of us, to think – at least not to think but to believe – that it was right. You didn't kick against anything, you just carried on. My mother used to say, You don't know when you're well off. When you was all small, Dad was working on a farm as a bailiff and he brought up the family – eight of us there was – on twelve bob a week. Well, I was earning 27/6d a week, so that was a great improvement to what they had.

—You were brought up to believe these things, but didn't there come a time when you stopped believing them? Politically, I mean . . .

No, I had no interest in politics, I never voted. It made no difference which party got in, they were only after their own ends and I'd still have to work for the same . . . Moreover, if Captain Fraser, who was a Conservative, had thought his gardener voted Labour he'd have probably told him to get out. There were places where all the workers had to vote Conservative or be sacked. And the workers always thought there might be some way the bosses could find out how they'd voted. We weren't educated enough to think different, we thought we'd be out of a job . . .

You returned to the charge. He must have felt the inequality, in fact he was constantly referring to it.

Course, there shouldn't be no difference, there shouldn't be no working class. The majority of these so-called gentry never work for their money, it's only been handed down. And there again, you see, if there was no workers there'd be no gentry. You've got to have workers to get gentry.

—Why do you say that?

Well, if every worker in the world stopped working, what would happen?

The gentry's money wouldn't do it any good. There shouldn't be no gentry. But if all their money was equally split up, before twelve months was out those with the best brains would have more than the others. You see, you must have monied people, you can't get on without money. I wouldn't mind having some myself, I wouldn't care what anybody thought of me.

—You mean you'd be happy to be one of the gentry.

I wouldn't say their ways, but I'd have some of their money. I would never get up in the high class. I don't like their ways. There's not much life in most of them, they just mope around. They don't go down to the local and enjoy a pint and a game of darts. Look at your father. He'd go out in the morning, come home at night, put his kilt on and sit there and smoke his pipe . . . I can't see it, I shouldn't like it, life would be very monotonous. The money side of it is all right, but the other side, no thank you . . .

Mrs Sells came in from shopping. Bert's ambivalences hung like a smokescreen in front of you. You turned the tape-recorder off. He was vanishing behind one of his jokes again, it was impossible to hold onto him. What did he mean? Gentry equals money, gentry shouldn't exist, monied people must always exist, resentment at their existence, nothing could change . . .

Do you drink this stuff? Mrs Sells slipped through the cluttered room with a couple of bottles of stout. It's about all he'll have nowadays . . . You thanked her and took the bottle, thinking to bring some with you next time. Bert ought to be pursued relentlessly into a corner of total consistency, instead of being left there smiling to himself as he opened the bottle, thinking no doubt that he'd strung you along.

You seen old Ilse? Mrs Sells asked, sitting down. A real good nanny she was, you know. What about the Carvells, do they still live in that bungalow up Ten Cottages way? . . . They had more sense than us, mother, not to get themselves into a tied cottage, Bert said, wiping his mouth. Old Bill Carvell used to think he was better class than us in the garden till we put him in his place . . .

You turned the recorder on.

—What did you think of him then?

A proper yes-sir man, he was, working day and night. Not like an ordinary groom who worked long hours on hunting days but otherwise did the least he could to make up. He was no good in the garden, he was supposed to help out in his spare time, like all decent grooms, but he'd just hang about the stables. You're a bloody fine one, you are, I said, why don't you give me a hand? . . . Oh, I've got something else to do . . . I'll smash you in the bloody ear in a minute then . . . But it never came to anything in the end.

—What about the other people who worked there? Johnson . . .

The butler. A smart little chap, I don't know what they paid him, probably got him cheap. But he was a sneaky little bugger, a proper News of the World. If you was in his good books he'd cop you half a pint of something, but if you wasn't in favour you'd get nothing for weeks, he wouldn't even speak. And then suddenly he'd start talking as though nothing had happened.

He was silly about Marie, you know, he'd let her dress up in his butler's trousers and jacket. They were about the same size and she looked a perfect butler. One day I went into the kitchen and there was Marie sitting on his lap. After five minutes Johnson said, Cor, bugger, I think you'd better get up, girl . . . It broke his heart when she left, although she got the bloody carving knife to him once. I don't know what happened . . .

When he was in a talkative mood, Johnson would tell Bert these things over a pint at the *Six Bells*. He never said much about the Manor, though, well, he wouldn't, would he? I mean, I was the riff-raff. And I wouldn't talk about it either, no one talked about where they worked in case something got back and you was out of a job.

—Did you go down to the pub much?

If I had a tanner in my pocket. I knew a bloke which was a very good darts player – well, I was too in those days. You'd go down to the tavern, beer was fourpence a pint, you'd buy half a pint and you could have a good evening winning half pints at darts. I used to take my old melodium up for a sing-song now and again. I learnt to play as a boy . . .

The pub had a slate club, he went on, where people paid in about 7d a week and when they were laid off sick they'd get 10s a week for so many weeks. After a time the government brought in the 'panel' – compulsory health insurance – that paid 15s a week but you didn't get the benefits until after three days off work and most blokes couldn't afford being off that long.

You saw him eyeing the clock above the fireplace, waiting to go to the pub where there was a darts match. There was time to slip in one more question at least. What about holidays, you asked.

Holidays! You must be kidding. I never had a holiday all the time I was there – only Bank Holidays and then, if I remember rightly, we had to go in on Good Friday till mid-day and had the Monday off . . . On a Sunday, he and the missus would push the pram down to *The Swan* and he'd go in to fetch a pint and a lemonade for her, and the kiddie would have a drink of his beer – brought up on it, she was – and then they'd come home.

—Not much entertainment then?

BBC – that's what I liked. Beer, bacco and crumpet. He chortled, looking again at the clock, and edged forward in his chair. It was late, the past was the past, there was nothing wrong in having a talk about it as long as it didn't interfere with the present. You unplugged the recorder and began to roll up the lead. Once the machine was put away people, as though released, sometimes said something important. You waited, but he said nothing.

There was still an hour to spare; the surprising convoy on the country lanes had delayed you less than you feared. Leaving the car, you walked through the churchyard behind the Manor and into the donkey paddock where, in the past, a number of ferocious brutes, as unwilling to have a child on their backs as you were to be mounted on them, had inflicted terror among the nettle patches. You hastened on over the style and along the footpath. Moments before, on a short cut from the motorway, a column of armoured lorries with motorcycle outriders, fire engines and police Range Rovers bristling with aerials had blocked the narrow road. After several miles, the convoy turned a familiar corner and, dark against the sky, you saw two mounds as large as prehistoric burial sites and a perimeter fence topped with barbed wire. The armoured lorries turned into a gate guarded by police. On the fence next to it a sign proclaimed: *Prohibited Place – Photographing and Sketching Forbidden*. Soon the convoy was swallowed up amidst the high earth banks and igloos and large buildings of the nuclear arms factory; and you drove on, a sense of anxiety pervading the memory of the country lane, no wider than when Bert used to chauffeur you and Ilse to tea parties at the Walkers (and down which, as the Morris 8 approached the little bridge, he'd accelerate, sending car and stomach flying up and laughter tumbling out as his hand steadied you in the front seat; while from the back Ilse's voice came sternly, I've told you before, Bert, that is dangerous . . . and the laughter was choked off despite Bert's grin as he adjusted his cap to a more rakish angle) . . .

The idea of following the footpath seemed suddenly pointless. The factory which lay directly in front had vanished again, as though swallowed by the rain-soaked land. What would you do at the perimeter fence? Nothing. You turned back through the graveyard and walked along the road bordering the Manor's kitchen garden. Somewhere, you recalled, a wicket gate once opened in this hedge. It was long since gone, for there was no sign of recent growth, but by the oak at the end of the garden a hole appeared. Jumping the ditch, you discovered that the view was obstructed by some sort of earth bank and pushed through to take cover behind it. Over the top you could make out the white walls of the old nursery and maids' rooms and below them the back door, kitchen and scullery. They were further away or smaller than you remembered, and the scullery door, where Bert and Carvell joined the maids for their morning tea had gone, it seemed. A woman came out of the back door with a basket and started to hang up laundry. You watched her, certain that she couldn't see you; for a moment wordless emotions drifted as indecipherably as a November fog across the retina of memory, sentient colours shimmered and vanished like a summer haze, leaving nothing. Shaking yourself free, you vanished in the way you had come . . .

The staff at the Manor didn't get together very much. At the Melbrays, for example, they had a servants' hall where the outdoor staff would go for a cup of tea. There were fourteen in the house alone, Carvell recalled, and none of them, not even the housekeeper, would sit down to tea until the butler came in. But there was no hall at the Manor and some of the staff were foreign. We English people never did like to work with foreigners. I don't know why but we always accepted an English person in preference.

—What did you think of Ilse?

She and I always got on, but I don't think that was true of the others. I'm sure Bert didn't. He used to spend an awful lot of time in his cottage when he should have been working. He had a grudge against Ilse, that I know, he probably resented her keeping an eye on him, as it were. And Ilse didn't trust Bert either, she used to speak sharp to him . . .

—You didn't think much of Bert, by the sound of it.

No, we were never bosom pals, as you'd call it. If Bert had been anything of a sport he'd have offered once in a while to see to the horses. Old
Winteringham would have, he was the old type of servant who knew that a
groom and a gardener worked together. I used to water the garden for Bert
in the summer, but he never gave anything back. I'm all right Jack, was
his attitude.

—The other day you said you were doing twice as much work as other
grooms. Didn't you ask for help?

Yes, what I really needed was a stable-lad. The Melbray's and the
Walker's grooms had boys. I asked Captain Fraser several times. He
always said, You've only got to ask me, I can always come out . . . Once in
a while after hunting he'd take the worst of the mud off the horses he'd
been riding. But he didn't make a habit of it. I don't think he liked the work
much. Oh my God, he'd say, this makes you sweat! . . . Then he'd light his
pipe and say, Well, I'd better get back to dinner now . . . And away he'd go.

Had he talked to Mrs Fraser direct, Carvell felt, he might have got a boy.
But he always asked the captain for anything he needed because he was the
governor. You'd better see Mrs Fraser about that, the captain always
answered; and when Carvell did – there was seldom a morning when she
didn't stop by to see the horses – he always got what he needed immediately. Invariably the cheques were signed by her; there was no shortage of
money there, it seemed, although the same wasn't true of his side. But the
captain never told him to ask her about the boy; and as time went on he no
longer bothered about it.

—Did he never provide money for anything?

Not to my knowledge. Your father was real Scotch, if I may say so . . .
Once, he had refused Carvell's urgent plea to replace the wire fence round
the paddock where they were keeping the foal bred from the beautiful dappled mare Mrs Fraser had brought from Germany. When Carvell walked
out one morning early to feed the colt he heard him whinnying and then,
to his horror, saw him hanging from an iron fence post with his guts trailing on the ground.

Carvell ran back to the house. On the lawn under their bedroom where
one of the French windows was always open, he whistled and shouted,
Hallo, there's trouble in the field! . . . It wasn't long before the captain
looked out. What the hell's up? Oh, all right, go on, I'll be down . . . Shortly

he appeared in the field with a coat over his pyjamas. Can we get him off?
...No, he's gone too far for that, Carvell replied... What did he want to
get himself into that bloody mess for? the captain exploded. And then he
shot him.

Mrs Fraser was very wild about it. There you are, Carvell told her, had
there been a proper post and rail fence the colt would have rolled off when
he tried to get across to the old mare in the next field... Oh yes, I realize it
was no fault of yours, she said... But Carvell, in all truth, never forgave
the captain.

Perhaps, you suggested, he had been reluctant to spend money that
wasn't his.

He wouldn't begrudge himself if it was something he really enjoyed. I'd
say they were in the top ten when it came to subscribing to hounds. There
were some who were more generous – the Huntleys would each give five
hundred guineas – but the Manor in all likelihood gave one hundred when
they could have hunted for twenty five guineas a season each.

—You reckon that they paid in hunt subscriptions about as much as
they paid you in a year...

Well, I never calculated it...

—Two pounds five shillings a week you got, that's £117 a year. One
hundred guineas is £105, isn't it?

Yes, that's right.

—And what would a hunter cost in those days?

One hundred, one hundred and twenty guineas was a fair price. A six-
year-old that would carry a lady side-saddle was worth anything up to 180
to 200 guineas. I don't expect they ever paid less than that.

—Did it never strike you that in a year you didn't earn the price of one of
their horses?

No. I'd been mixing with these people all my life. The more money the
gentry had the better we liked them in my father's business. The price of a
horse depended on their means to a fair extent...

Throughout he betrayed no surprise or resentment at the comparisons
you'd drawn. Everything about him was gentle, as though the mute animal world in which he dealt had sheltered him from other realities.

You changed tack: until he became a groom at the Manor he had always hunted. Had he not regretted no longer being able to do so.

But no, he had hunted every Monday when the captain went to London on business in the first few years. He would pilot Mrs Fraser, as it was called, opening any awkward gates and that sort of thing. Not that it happened very often because if the horses would jump it they'd be the first across. Mrs Fraser really loved a day's hunting. At first, being used to school riding and drag-hunting, she had been surprised that the women could last out the whole day. But soon she had come to realize that, like their horses, they were bred to it, and it wasn't long before she was equalling them in endurance. She was a marvellous horsewoman with wonderful hands. Horses always went kindly for her, she had only to talk to her mount to get him to go where she wanted.

She was the idol of his eye on a horse, he exclaimed. It was a great honour to put her up in the saddle. She looked perfect in every way. Her position in the saddle, a nice straight back, her navy-blue habit, a silk top hat on Thursdays, a bowler on Mondays, a veil. She wore a lemon-coloured stock and it was always correctly tied and went with her hair. She looked, everyone said so, a real picture sitting side-saddle on the dappled grey mare. Horse and rider seemed to have come out of a bandbox. Other ladies could be dressed the same but they didn't look the part because they weren't horsewomen.

—When you were out with her did you feel any distinctions made because you were the groom?

No. I was riding in the captain's place, as it were. Where she went I went, and I wasn't always behind—

But that's not what he's asking, Mrs Carvell interjected. William can never see class distinctions. He was made to feel embarrassed sometimes. At the meet he'd be with the grooms...

—What class distinctions did you see, Mrs Carvell?

Well, we wouldn't go to the Hunt Ball, for instance. William had gone before, but now he was a groom it was different. He's too conservative, he'll always cover up. I didn't give a damn. I always felt myself to be as good as them, just as educated. The Rhondda where I come from is a mining area, but it's also a place where people are very keen on sending their children to school. My father was in charge of the pit ponies which was a cut above the ordinary miner. We were the better middle class, do you know what I mean? We never knew the gentry because the people who owned the mines didn't live there. And as a nurse I met very few people who didn't appreciate that, as a professional woman, I had something that they perhaps hadn't got.

—Weren't you all the more struck by the contrast? After all, here was a situation where almost everything revolved round the gentry...

No. I accept life as it comes, high, low or indifferent. I never begrudged or envied them. That was their life and it didn't bother me. The only thing – and that was personal – was the many times when I felt William was hurt. That was the only thing...

Do you get any hunting these days, old boy? He looks through the fogged car window; the rain has stopped and a rolling countryside under a lightening sky has replaced the wet flatlands of the Kennet valley.

His hand fumbles in a pocket and produces a grey handkerchief. Awkwardly with his left hand he clears a patch of mist, rubbing as though to dry the raindrops on the outside of the window.

I used to enjoy it down in Devon. Father never rode, d'you know? Stealthily, his hand drops back to his pocket, brings out his wallet. Through the cleared patch of window the rain-soaked land appears in strident browns and greens. He counts the notes, returns the wallet. I have nobody left who has my ambitions, have I?

—You were saying that the Manor seemed like a community. Were things different in the other houses, Eileen?

In some, I should think. Not all the people that used to come to dinner parties at the Manor would treat their servants like we were. There was a definite class distinction between the uppers and workers in some houses. That was the recognized thing then.

—Why was the Manor different? They were uppers, weren't they?

Yes. But they never struck me like that. You were never given the impression that you were there only to clean. As long as you got on and did the work everything was fine. The staff was always on the go because it was a big house – an old house, with atmosphere, Eileen thought. Comfortable – cosy, that was the word . . . Although there was one thing that wasn't cosy at all. Once when they were spring-cleaning late in the evening she went up to the tower room to shut the window. As she entered she suddenly felt very cold, her hair stood on end and somebody touched her lightly on the shoulder. She looked, half expecting to see Doris. But no, there was nobody. She turned and ran, and half way down the stairs fell and rolled down the rest. The others came to see what was wrong. They'll think I'm mad, she said to herself, I can't tell them. Then she remembered dining-room conversations in which guests laughingly asked Mrs Fraser whether she had seen *her* lately. And once she heard her reply, Yes, I saw her the other day coming down the stairs . . .

When Eileen told her, your mother said that years ago, so the story went, the sixteen-year-old daughter of the Manor's owners had fallen in love with a stable boy. When her father found out he shut her in the tower room and there she had starved herself to death. Her ghost, long-haired and dressed in a flowing gown, would come down the big staircase and walk out of the front door. She won't hurt you, Mrs Fraser said to me as though she accepted the ghost as part of the house. But I never went up to the tower room again . . .

You laughed. Ghosts, real and imaginary, of the past . . . But she hadn't answered the question: why had the servants been treated differently at the Manor. Was it perhaps because your mother was American.

It probably was, yes. It hadn't occurred to me before. She wasn't a British snob, because some of them were very snobby – and still are. I often had little talks with her when I went to turn down her bed. I could always talk freely, ask her advice. She was a very sweet lady, you couldn't call her anything else.

—You said last time that you got on well with the indoor staff. What about Bert and Mr Carvell?

I liked Bert most. He was very fatherly, always ready to listen and help if I was worried about something. He took Doris and me under his wing. His wife was a nice, motherly woman and they both made me feel welcome if I wanted a chat . . . But Carvell, no, she would never have thought of going over to the stables. There was something about him she instinctively disliked; he seemed a bit of a womanizer.

—What makes you say that?

He passed a remark about me in the pub once which Bert overheard. He said he bet he'd only have to say the word and I'd go out with him, I was a lovely girl. He didn't know Bert was in the pub . . .

Bert, Interview 3, page 5

Johnson heard what he said, so did I. Cor, I wouldn't half like to kiss her – only it wasn't exactly kiss he said. It was out in the stableyard and of course the butler goes straight in and tells them what Carvell said. The governor was up in bloody arms, he came down to the bottom of the garden to fetch me. I had to go into the smoking room . . .

Carvell, Interview 5, page 17

I didn't know anything about it until Mrs Sells came across to the stables and pulled my leg about Eileen. What do you mean? I said. Well, according to Bert, you're getting fresh with her . . . I don't mind what's said, I answered, I'm not guilty . . . Then one day, without mentioning what was brewing, the captain summoned me, Bert and Johnson into the smoke room. Bert repeated a yarn he'd put about that I'd said I wanted to kiss and sleep with Eileen when she brought the tea over to the harness room . . .

Bert

When the governor called me in he said: What did you hear Carvell say? . . . I don't like to tell you in front of madam, sir . . . It's all right, Bert, she said, I'll put my fingers in my ears . . . Come on, the governor said . . . And I had to say it, though I didn't want to get Carvell into a row, because Johnson had already told him. If the governor found one bloody thing different from what Johnson said we'd both be for it. He was bloody foaming at the mouth. I'll sack the bloody lot of you, he said, clear the lot out to get to the right one – who's right and who's wrong. He kept talking round and round trying to catch us out . . .

Carvell

I denied the whole thing. Then the captain said he was calling in Eileen's father, and I said, Fetch him in . . . He was the village policeman. When he came in, Captain Fraser said, Carvell doesn't accept this story at all . . .

Bert

The trouble was Carvell denied it right to the end. Carvell fancied the ladies, you know. It was the sort of thing I'd have said myself dozens of times, but not in front of someone like that butler bloke. Actually, the governor was on Carvell's side, thought me and Johnson was ganging up on him . . .

Carvell

Well, can we have Eileen come in? her father said. The captain rang. She looked very surprised to see us all in there. I want to ask you if you've anything against Mr Carvell here, he said. No, not at all, he's always been a perfect gentleman as far as I'm concerned . . .

Eileen

—Do you remember what you said?

No, I wasn't called in at all . . .

Bert

She came in but I don't remember what she had to say. I was too bloody scared. What was going to happen if the governor said, here's a week's pay in lieu of notice, bloody get out . . .

Carvell

Then she went out and Captain Fraser said, There you are. Now look here, I don't want to hear any more of this. If I do there's going to be trouble – and that was meant for whom it hurt most . . .

Bert

In the end he let us go and no more was heard of it. That was the one and only really bad time I had with the governor . . .

Eileen

My father went and spoke to Carvell and he apologized, said it was the beer talking, he hadn't really meant it. My dad asked me if he had made any advances. No, I said, he hadn't. I never had much to do with him . . .

Carvell   ·

Later on her father knocked on the harness-room door. I'm sorry this has happened, he said, but I'm pleased to hear the result. It was Captain Fraser who wanted to push it . . . Well, I replied, you'd believe your own daughter, wouldn't you? . . . After that we were friends.

Eileen

—So that was the reason you disliked Carvell?

No, I never liked him before that. He always made me feel uneasy. He was a placid enough man, but he had a prima donna type of wife and he probably needed the company of a warm woman . . .

Carvell

I didn't speak to Bert for a very long time after that. The reason he spread that story about was that he thought we might move into the stable cottage if Mrs Winteringham moved out. Bert was a very jealous chap, you know, he wanted that cottage very badly. He'd go round at night and tap on the window to frighten the old girl. I was in the harness-room next to the cottage one night when he did it . . .

Bert

I was disappointed over the cottage, yes. They let old Mrs Winteringham stay on, through pity I suppose, but it really annoyed me because I was there all those years and Winteringham had been there only a couple of years before he died. Even then, you know, the governor took her front room, the best room, boarded it across and turned it into a harness-room. The old gal was left with a bit about two foot six across. She had to agree, she hadn't a leg to stand on because it was a tied cottage.

—What was your cottage like?

A pigsty when we went in, you could shovel up the filth after the old basket-maker had moved. Originally it was part of a coach-house. The big bedroom only had sheets of asbestos stuff for a ceiling. Freezing cold it was. The place was lousy with mice, I'd put a trap down and they were so small and starved they'd eat the cheese without springing the trap. Other times I'd set traps in the bedroom and we'd swing up at night with a candlestick in our hands and get into bed and *bang bang bang* they'd go, one after another.

—Did you ever ask for improvements?

No, you didn't dare, really. The majority of cottages around never had running water or bathrooms. An outdoor Elsan for a lavatory was normal enough. At the start of the war, when your mother had the coach-house turned into cowstalls, we got light and water. Before that, though, I was young and wanting to get married, and it was the first place we had together. I was happy enough with it and the job . . .

Eileen

—You liked Bert, disliked Carvell, said the other day you had a row with Ilse —

She was the only person in the house I didn't get on with. We weren't enemies but we used to clash. She was a good and devoted nanny, no doubt about that, but there was something severe about her that would frighten children, I used to think. She could try to be domineering — but I wouldn't stand for that. It made me cross, though, that she and Marie always spoke in German because I thought they were saying things they didn't want us to know . . .

Not that things were always that smooth between them. Eileen was in the kitchen one day when Ilse blustered in without knocking. She said something and Marie picked up a plate of food and said, Get out of my kitchen, you German swine! . . . Ilse turned and went out quicker than she'd come in and the plate hit the door. Marie! Eileen cried . . . *Grrrrr*! Marie replied, and Eileen thought she had better get out too. The trouble between them, she believed, was because Hitler invaded Austria and took it over, didn't he? . . .

One day in 1938 when everyone thought there was going to be war, Ilse said to her, My führer would love you with your blue eyes and fair hair . . . It wasn't said in a nasty way and Eileen thought maybe Ilse was jealous because she was blonde. But later she remembered the remark and thought she hadn't been wrong. Ilse was always talking about the führer, there could be no doubt that she was a spy.

—A spy! What made you think that?

It seemed fate. Whenever I heard the phone ringing and no one answered, I'd go to the extension by the kitchen door. If I heard the captain speaking, I'd put the receiver down. But many's the time I came by and found Ilse with the receiver off. She'd put it back quick when she saw me. I was sure she was spying on him because he was in the army . . .

You laughed.

She/He/She

Whatever happened to Janey, old boy? Did she die?
Yes.
Oh!
Silence, only the sound of tyres zipping on the wet black
surface. Is it possible? Has he forgotten everything?
Do you remember Ilse?
Ilse?
Yes.
Oh, she was the officer who ran our lives in a manner of
speaking, wasn't she?
Really?
His eyes express bewilderment, fearing a mistake. She wore
a uniform and was stern with us, wasn't she?
That's right, she was . . .

—Would you say she was more strict than the other nannies you came
across, Bert?

Oh yes. Because she was German, I suppose. A real regimental nurse,
stomped along in proper military fashion. A damned good nurse, though,
exceptionally good and smart. She looked after you as good as anyone
could. Had you corrected as you should be. She only had to talk a bit strict
and you was good. Poor old devil, I used to think – about you, I mean. My
kiddies used to have their own way a bit more than you. But you always
seemed very happy with her, never cried to go with your mother . . .

—What did you think of her yourself?

To speak the truth, we didn't get on. The other maids I could always have a chat and a bit of fun with, but Ilse didn't mix. It looked as though she classed herself better than the others. She'd pass the time of day with Mrs Winteringham and Mrs Carvell, and she was always over in the stables with Carvell, but she'd never come round with the poor old gardener, or up to my place. High and mighty, I had the feeling with her that I shouldn't speak unless spoken to . . .

Almost every day Ilse would stop by at Mrs Carvell's when she took the children out for a walk. Mrs Carvell admired her smartness, her almost Parisian elegance when she was out of uniform. On her afternoons off, Ilse would go to Mrs Carvell's and they'd play cards. Newmarket and that sort of thing, for 1½d per 36, nothing high-brow. Life was different in those days, Mrs Carvell recalled, they had to make their own entertainment.

Much as she liked her, Mrs Carvell found Ilse irritating at times. She was fanatical about cleanliness, made her own life a misery by cleaning. Even at Mrs Carvell's she'd go into the kitchen and start clearing up. Oh, leave it, Ilse, I'd say, but she couldn't help herself. Once she said, You know, Hitler is marvellous but he talks too much, he's going too far . . . Well, Ilse, so do you sometimes, I said, laughing . . . You don't mean it, she replied . . . But I did.

Though she was an intelligent woman, Mrs Carvell went on, she was not very sensitive to other's feelings, and made no bones about her disapproval of most things English. Particularly of the way nannies looked after their children. Nanny Walker came in for criticism because she didn't mind how dirty her children got. Ilse wouldn't stand for that, you had to be clean at all times and she changed your clothes several times a day. And whereas most nannies spent time playing with the children, Ilse, Mrs Carvell noted, felt that she was there to work, not to play . . . All the same, you know, she was marvellous to you, it was she who really brought you up. She did everything for you, was like a mother to you. And she was a very trustworthy person to have in the house because she was very loyal to your mother, very fond of her. Not that she was past rebuking her either, if she felt like it.

—Rebuking her? How?

She'd order your mother out of the nursery or keep her from coming in if she didn't want her there. I saw it happen once. If your mother did something she didn't approve of, got you some clothes or a toy she didn't like, especially one that made a noise, she'd shrug her shoulders in a special way and say, Well! . . . A noisy toy wasn't a little gentleman's toy, you see, and she'd go on about it until your mother changed it.

—Ilse dominated her pretty much then . . .

Not dominated, no, but let her know who was in charge in the nursery. She didn't want your mother, let alone your father, to have anything much to do with you, I think. She wouldn't let you run downstairs on your own to see them, she had to lead you by the hand. If you were dirty she felt guilty. Up to the age of four you wore white – lovely silk blouses, I remember – and even after that you were never dressed in anything rough. You had to be a little lord Fauntleroy, it was part of being a good English nanny for Ilse and she didn't want to fail. She had a thing about bringing you up as a perfect little gentleman – but she carried it a bit far because she didn't know what it really meant.

—Did she say any of this?

Oh yes, it was her duty, her business. She obviously felt that this was your father's wish and as she was never quite sure of herself where he was concerned – although she never said that – she didn't want to give him the slightest satisfaction of criticising her. Never to be put in the wrong. So she was always on the ready with you . . .

Often your father went days without saying a word to Ilse other than good morning. At breakfast he disappeared behind his newspaper. After, if it wasn't a hunting day, he went to his study and continued to read the paper. He had given up going to London when the office of the German shipping agents he had opened proved unsuccessful, she didn't know why. Now he occupied himself solely with sport. Ilse was sometimes surprised that he could live without doing anything really useful, but he seemed quite happy. He was a man – first and foremost a gentleman – without a modern idea in his head, she thought.

—What do you mean by saying he was a gentleman?

To begin with in the way he treated the servants as human beings. Of course, he liked to feel that the lower classes looked up to him and to his social circle. He got a lot of satisfaction from that. But he was always very nice to me. When he made himself a cup of tea at 5 a.m. before going out riding in Hamburg he always offered me one, and that seemed an unexpected human touch of employer to employee. And when the cook had her day off and I cooked the evening meal he would offer me a cocktail. Oh, a woman who doesn't take alcohol is no good, he'd say when I refused . . .

—And as a man?

What shall I say? He was someone who would take any risk to satisfy his pleasure. Would he have married a wife twelve or thirteen years younger otherwise and let her money give him everything he wanted?

—Is that what you thought? That he married her for money?

I often thought that was part of the reason. He was very much in love with her though, there always seemed to be a lot of laughter and happiness between them. Not that he spoiled her much with love and attention. I never saw him kiss or embrace her. When they were together in the evening he sat in his chair and hid behind the *Times*. He seemed a bit selfish, a bit lazy. Don't you think that when men get to forty they become a bit lazy like that?

—I don't know, I've only just got there. I thought he liked women.

Oh yes, he was – how would you say? – a lady's man. He could be charming with women, he had a way with them . . . So much so, she went on, that a regrettable incident had occurred on arrival in England. At the small country hotel where they had been staying while the house was being got ready he had met a young South African woman whom he had insisted must be the first guest at the Manor. Ilse took little notice at first but soon it became apparent that he was having an affair with her. She was indiscreet and the servants all knew . . . We'd been at the Manor only a few weeks when your mother took you and me back to Germany with her. She gave no reason, just said we were going to live with her mother who was still there. It seemed such a sad thing to happen when they had come to make a new home and everything should have been happy . . .

After several weeks apart, your mother returned to the Manor alone.

—And that was the end of it?

When we returned some time later the woman had gone. Everything was all right then, I think. I heard from Mrs Carvell once that he had an affair with his manicurist. I didn't want to know about it, I felt sad because your mother was such a lovely young woman . . .

—What did you make of him?

I didn't like him as much as your mother, especially because of the way he treated his horses. He was too severe, he lost his temper with them. A lot of horses used to throw him because of it . . . One day coming home from hunting the captain's horse just humped its shoulders neat as anything and off he came, hitting his back on a tree. Carvell, who knew from the way he had been touching the horse with his spur that something would happen, looked down and laughed. Glowering on the ground the captain retorted, It's all bloody fine for you . . . Well, Carvell said, you've been asking for it . . . When it came to horses he always spoke his mind.

And he was always asking for it. To Carvell's annoyance he insisted on using real spurs instead of the dummies purposely laid out for him with his boots. Wanting to be in front of everyone else, he asked ridiculous things of a horse no brave man would ask; and when the horse failed he swore at it instead of blaming himself. The other grooms noticed and said, He's a hard bloke on a horse . . . In fact, Carvell thought, he was a bully who rode like a soldier on a very short rein whereas a bold hunting man would give his horse freedom. He was envious of his wife who rode with a long rein, who'd just drop her hand and *whoosh* her horse would fly over places that others wouldn't jump. His horses went for him out of fright – fright of the spurs – and nothing else.

Sometimes Carvell felt that the captain was taking out his own inadequacies on his horses. Although he was often domineering and sarcastic, he would also appear nervous, standing by the stables kicking his riding boots as though he wanted to say something but wasn't sure whether he ought. Carvell felt that he was never totally happy. Perhaps it had to do with riding because otherwise he was very polite. All the beaters and keepers at the shooting parties always had a good word for him. He was probably very generous to them because he preferred shooting to hunting, Carvell thought. There was no doubt about it, he was a gentleman all right.

—A man who never achieved any of his ambitions, I'd say, an embittered failure. But that's another matter. What makes a gentleman in your view?

Manners is the first thing, I'd say. A gentleman has to be polite, treat you on the same level as himself. He couldn't treat you like dirt. You could always tell a gentleman by that, and by his way of talking.

—And money?

Well, a country gentleman would have to have money to be looked up to in those days. Those who gave when they were asked were thought more of in the village than the others . . . A retired clergyman, the Rev. Thesby, who had returned to his Georgian family house on the hill overlooking the Manor, was the most important gentleman in the village in this respect, Carvell continued. The villagers knew they could go to him in difficulty. The old, the infirm, the poor could count on a hundredweight of coal, fruit and groceries at Christmas. His generosity was rivalled only by Mr Curling, who was often considered the village squire because of his gifts which included the land to build the village school. And then, though they lived half a dozen miles away in the county's most splendid Elizabethan house, a palace of a place, there were the Bunyons who were highly respected because they owned most of the farming land for miles round and were considered to be good to their labourers.

How many large houses were there in the immediate vicinity, you asked.

He began to list the familiar names: Wooton Hall, Nefton Court, Sherman's Wood, Beech Park, Firlands, Pember House . . . and they echoed through you, constrained and nervous, with the sounds of children, nannies and parents at tea parties, dancing classes, hunt meets, tennis lessons . . . Fifteen or sixteen within a five mile radius, he concluded.

—And how did the Manor, or rather its owners, compare?

They were well respected, I'd say, but they didn't live up to what the village expected of the Manor House. It should have been the main house and held garden fêtes and flower-shows every year, organized the Mother's Union and the Women's Institute, that's what the people wanted. But your parents didn't put themselves out really. They seemed outside the village in some way. I mean, look at the Melbrays. Sir Harold had been brought up to mix with the village people, he knew the men by their Christian names, supported the local football and cricket clubs and went to their dinners, even if they were in the back parlour of a pub. Lady Melbray was active in the Women's Institute, the Girl Guides and the dramatic club. When they went through the village they were treated as nobility, everyone touched their cap . . .

—Perhaps the Frasers seemed outsiders because they were new to the village . . .

I don't think so. Look at the Winchesters, that American family who had settled in the village even more recently. They involved themselves actively in local life. Mrs Winchester was Chairman of the Women's Institute for years, the oldest daughter, Cristina, took up the nursing side of the village and another daughter was Guides leader. They held a Christmas party each year for the village children, talked to everyone in the local shop, knew everyone's name and became very popular. Your mother could have counted on two hands the number of people she knew in the village. She never set foot in our house, for example, whereas Mrs Winchester would call in on her groom's wife. Your father was more of a mixer, it's true. He belonged to the British Legion and helped on the local Conservative party committee. But that was about the extent of it . . .

You must remember, Mrs Carvell put in, that your mother was very shy – too shy to be in the public eye. On the other hand, your father was a very nice gentleman who always made you feel at ease. He could talk to anyone and wasn't stand-offish. A very charming, courteous man.

—Really? That's not exactly the impression I've just been getting . . .

I always thought he was very nice, I liked him. Of course, he was a lady's man but it wasn't entirely his fault because the women used to throw themselves at him. You couldn't imagine a young woman finding Sir Harold appealing – he was a bit of an old bore, really – or any of the other men who only thought about horses. No, your father was the only catch and the women noticed him because he was an outsider. Lady Blount told me several times how charming she found him. And Lady Melbray said the same.

—I don't think Ilse did . . .

No, she didn't, she was always on the defensive with him and he with her. He knew she was watching him like a hawk. She knew all about the South African woman, she'd seen him and her once or twice in a – what shall I say? – clasp. Ilse was very quiet on her feet, she could be in and out before they'd seen her. She used to tell me about it. And, as I said before, Ilse was very loyal to your mother . . .

—And what did *she* think, do you know?

I don't, no. All I can say is that she seemed crazy about him, especially when they first came here. It was always Alexander darling this, Alexander darling that. A devoted couple, I'd say, for the first few years. Before they got married her mother sent her on a world cruise to forget him, didn't she? She didn't want her to marry him because he was divorced and a lot older than her. Mrs Winteringham told me, your mother must have told her because she was very friendly and at ease with her. She must have married him when she was twenty, didn't she?

—Twenty-one. He was thirteen years older. He could turn the charm on and off, couldn't he? I don't remember much of it, that's for sure . . .

Oh yes, she had seen the other side of it, heard him a few times in the stables going hell for leather at her, shouting until she started to cry. As she walked away he'd say, Blasted woman, and turn away in a huff. He was bad-tempered, Mrs Carvell believed, because he was the underdog, had to kowtow to her because she had the money. Whereas she, a young girl fascinated by something about an older man, wanted him to take the lead which he couldn't because he lacked the money.

Speeding now deliberately past the familiar turn-off and the sign that indicates the village, hoping the old man won't notice, won't protest that he wants to go home, home on his own where he'll never go again. Cruel day.

His lips move, spelling out the letters that have sped into the rear mirror before he can mutter them. Knowing without knowing, blankly staring, his eyes begin to water again. The blankness penetrates like a fog, anaesthetizing the nerve ends, thank God.

Vengeful day, when sons become the father of their fathers, without forethought. How should we know?

His hand feels in his pocket. Have I any friends left, old boy?

—I always thought it was he who was responsible for everything that went wrong, Ilse. But it's she I really can't come to terms with, even now she'd dead. She seems nebulous...

Nebulous?... Yes, I think I know what you mean, Ronnie. Although she always seemed happy and gay, there was a remoteness, a distance about her that I could never bridge. I got so close and no closer. To begin with I didn't notice it because I had this wonderful feeling of being with a lovely young woman. Her complexion, her naturally curly dark blond hair, her slenderness, the way she carried herself impressed me. But as I came to know her better I felt she was someone who had led a very sheltered life. I came to feel almost maternal towards her – and yet I was only two years older! But by then I had been working for nine years and I knew, in a way that she couldn't, how life can knock you about. She seemed still to be under her mother's tutelage, too young to be a mother herself...

In answer to a question, Ilse went on to describe that formidable, slightly ridiculous, exorbitant woman, your grandmother, who had left her native Colorado for a life of semi-exile with her second husband, a penurious German baron, shortly before the first World War. Very wealthy in her own right, the baroness, as she was proud to be known, dominated husband and the three children from her first marriage with an energy as unstaunchable as her flow of talk.

Rather tall, with beautiful white curly hair framing a full face, blue eyes and a small mouth, she was an imposing woman, Ilse remembered. She adorned herself with masses of jewellery and ridiculous hats at which she herself sometimes laughed... Ilse, this one is the absolute end, isn't it? she exclaimed when the hat, decorated with a large bird, proved too wide to allow her to get into the car.

Possessive of all her family, the baroness was particularly possessive of her youngest daughter, Janey. Almost every day in Hamburg she came to whisk her off on shopping expeditions, Ilse remembered. The baroness loved shopping. Oh, she would say, we must go into town to buy sugar, it's a pfennig cheaper... How strange, Ilse thought, that this tremendously wealthy lady considered it worth taking her chauffeur-driven Cadillac into town to save a pfennig on sugar! But then, there was no doubt about it, the baroness was a bit mean. Although she never descended to the kitchen in her own vast town house, never gave orders to the cook face to face but telephoned them down to the basement, the baroness knew exactly what was left over... Even if it's only the smallest piece of meat, the cook told Ilse. Her meanness was passed on in instructions to her daughter, which meant that there was never much dinner left over for Ilse and the cook after their employers had eaten.

—Did my mother ever talk to you about her life?

No, she never opened herself to me, I knew only that she had spent the first World War in Germany, nothing more. She never asked me questions about my past either. I wouldn't say she wasn't interested, but there was a distance between us. She was the lady and I was – not the servant because she didn't treat me as one – but there was this difference. I used to think, these people aren't interested in you, all that matters is that you do your job. In any case, I didn't want to allow myself to be swallowed up by the family like most English nannies . . .

Pursuing an image of your mother, you ignored Ilse's train of thought and asked whether life as lady of the house at the Manor had satisfied Janey.

To begin with, yes, Ilse replied. She loved the riding, was happy that her husband could lead the life he wanted. She wasn't critical or demanding; if anything she was too tolerant, especially of the staff. As long as the rooms looked presentable, as long as the dinner-table was set as she wanted, she seemed content. To Ilse's surprise, the Manor was never properly spring-cleaned. On one occasion, when your mother was abroad, Ilse turned out her wardrobe; among the clothes she found a white fox stole which had been completely eaten by moths . . . But she didn't like giving orders, Ronnie. She was so nice to everyone that they took to her very easily. Except for Mrs Carvell – she and your mother didn't get on, I remember. Although she was so nice, I felt it was a long time before she overcame being her mother's daughter and developed her own personality. She was very shy and extremely feminine – she had a feminine attitude to marriage . . .

—What's a feminine attitude to marriage?

It's terrible how I analyse your mother and father, isn't it? By feminine I mean wanting very much to be married, feeling that without a husband you are only half a person. Not that her femininity meant softness. She never seemed a very emotional person. During that unfortunate incident with your father when we returned to Germany, she showed no suffering, no emotion at all. Perhaps she repressed her feelings. But she always appeared calm, even-tempered, gay – no, that isn't the word, *frölich* – yes, there was a cheerfulness about her that I liked.

It was three or four years before she began to develop her own personality, Ilse thought. At first she accepted her husband's attitudes uncritically; but later she began to assert her own ideas. Perhaps their different cultural backgrounds played a part in this. Ilse noticed it first when your mother insisted, against your father's wishes, that you and she eat with them in the dining room. And again when she refused your father's express determination to send you away to boarding-school at seven . . . I don't want Ronnie to be like other English children and leave home so early, she told Ilse, who agreed, thinking that it was terrible to send a child away so young.

With a shiver of appreciation, you asked whether Janey had ever said more about her opposition to boarding-school.

Not really. Sending children away wasn't the custom in America and Germany and she didn't believe it was necessary for a good education. Sooner or later, though, she knew you would have to go away, but I thought it wouldn't be until public school at thirteen.

—Do you think she had any particular ideas on bringing up children?

She wasn't the sort of person who would say to a nanny, You must do this or that. She was very generous in that way and I think she trusted me . . .

—Ilse says, Mrs Carvell, that you and my mother didn't get on . . .

It was mutual, we didn't like each other. She was a charming, sweet person really, but she was uncomfortable with me. I think it was because I had my hackles up all the time at the way she treated William. I don't say she wasn't a lady, but she never spoke to me the way your father did, never came to the house even at Christmas.

—Perhaps she was frightened of you in some way.

I can't understand it. I know a lot of people call me Sergeant Major to this day. Your mother was very nervous, she'd blush scarlet when anybody talked to her, it was quite embarrassing. She must have had some mental worry to make her like that, mustn't she?

—I don't know. I suppose she was inexperienced in the way of life here . . .

Yes, Mrs Carvell agreed, perhaps that was why she had never seemed to settle at the Manor. The gentry used to comment on how much time she spent abroad. She's very nice, they'd say, but she's always away. Up to two months each winter in Switzerland skiing during the best of the hunting season, too. It wasn't the done thing. At most the gentry took a summer house for a fortnight on the Isle of Wight with the children and nanny . . . In the end I felt she was as much a stranger when she left as when she arrived . . .

—Yes . . . You and she were strangers to this valley where the mist rose from the low-lying fields or dripped from low-lying clouds; yes, strangers in this bog of 'county' conventions, gentlemanly rituals, parochialism: did she not deride them? Yes, for their owners' lack of interest in anything beyond their horses' nose, I remember it well . . . Strangers here at home, at home where you were strangers: in the sharp Alpine air, the sun glinting on the snow, the slow climb up on skins, the fast descent . . . Skiing together meant freedom, independence . . .

Increasingly she began to assert her will, Ilse recalled. After Colin was born in 1936, and again the following winter, she decided to go skiing alone with you. Your father felt he was getting too old. The third winter she took Colin, Ilse and you. After a short time in the smart hotel where she always stayed, she moved to a small pension owned by the parents of one of her ski instructors . . . I don't think she'd have done this if your father had been there. It seemed to me a decisive step on her part, as if she were saying, All right, I've got my own ideas and wishes now and I'm going to carry them out.

—Why did she move, did she have more friends there?

She said she preferred it, it was nearer the slopes. Our room was in a different wing to hers. When we left at the end of the stay, we went to the station by sleigh and she walked with the ski instructor. Only then, as they came into the station, did I guess that they were having an affair. Knowing your father I thought, Why shouldn't she? To tell the truth, I never spoke to anyone about it or ever thought about it again . . .

Of course, you told yourself, there was another, more important reason why she was a stranger at the Manor: your father . . . They didn't get on, that was why she spent a lot of time abroad. The 'county' was secondary,

its ways parochial but not alien to someone brought up in an urban international circle where the same basic views and prejudices were held, only
with more wit, polish and breadth . . .

—Did you get the impression, Bert, that she was at ease with strangers
— strangers, say, of the working class?

I don't expect she ever saw them, did she? I've been round the front
weeding or something and people have come to the front door – salesmen,
travellers, people selling pegs, flowers. The maid would come out and say,
Go round the back to see the cook. Your mother would take no notice of
them. Not only your mother, other people were the same, they're all tar-
red with the same brush. Lady Melbray, she was a bit haughty, I know
that. I don't think she'd ever even notice me in the car when I drove you
over there. But your mother would always say, Drive careful, Bert, or
something like that. Not Lady Melbray, she'd have got the whip out if she
could. That's what her chauffeur-groom used to reckon, anyhow.

I'll say that, though, I always liked your mother, even though she never
said much to me in those years before the war. As a young woman I
thought she was lovely. On a horse especially. I've never known her really
upset. I never gave her cause to be. I did my work and if she said, Pick me
up in the car at three o'clock, I was there. I never had a row with her all the
time I was at the Manor. And I always thought she was happy with your
father. The way they spoke to one another – it was always, darling this and
darling that. Which maybe doesn't mean a thing – no more than me saying my missus is a silly old devil. But I shouldn't think you talk like that if
you don't think something of someone, surely.

No, Ronnie, I don't believe she had any idea at all how other people
lived. I was very fond of her, she was the idol of my eye on a horse as you
know, but I don't think she could imagine what we had to do to live . . .
One morning out exercising the horses with her, Carvell recalled, a
pheasant flew up out of a ditch. Her Alsatian jumped to catch it. Carvell
hopped off his horse quick as a flash to take the pheasant from the dog and
pull its neck . . . What are you going to do with that? she asked . . . Well, he
replied, *that* will go into the pot . . . But you can't eat it, William, she said,
it hasn't been shot . . . Shot or not, it'll be in the pot on Sunday . . . And she
answered, Well, I think the dogs ought to have it . . . Ignoring her, he put
the bird in his purchase pocket and they continued on their ride.

—You mean, because it hadn't been shot you couldn't—?

She seemed surprised that I should grab it. As she could buy anything she wanted, I think she thought we could all do the same. Which we definitely couldn't. I remember I used to go to a fellow on a farm here and get rabbits for 9d each. He'd give you two for a shilling which was very reasonable and we were glad to get them. But your mother wouldn't have any idea about that sort of thing . . .

You

Well, this is where we're going to stop.
Ah!
Do you want to get out then?
He limps up to the front door on his stick. Mrs S., the matron greets him and shows him to his room as though he has been there before. In the hall, a grey-haired wraith stares soundlessly at him.
He sits in a chair. The sun shines through the window, shines on the roses in the garden beyond. After a time he says, Well, old boy, I'd better be getting home.
You're going to be staying here for a while, Alexander.
Oh! His eyes show fear.
They'll look after you properly, see that you get enough to eat. You can't go on alone any more. You need company . . .
I'll just walk then, old boy.
You're a long way away, I'm afraid. Look, I've unpacked your things. Everything will be all right. I'll come by tomorrow. Take care of yourself.
Sitting in the chair he starts to cry.

—Even now there's a distance, Ilse, an intangible barrier which restrains me. I can't get close to him, can't find real feelings. I fear him because I'm like him, fearful of leaping through the barrier to discover myself . . .

I can understand that, Ronnie, it grew from this early lack of relationship. I don't remember him ever picking you up or playing with you. I'm not interested in my child, he said to me once, until he can go out shooting with me...I don't think I ever heard him say hello to you and at meal times he didn't talk. When you were about a year old, your mother asked me to put you in the playpen in the living room when he came home for lunch. He walked in, sat down in his chair without noticing you and buried himself behind his newspaper. I thought it was terrible...

—Totally distant, no?

Well, I don't want to give the impression that he disowned you. I remember him laughing once or twice with me about something you said. Like the time you told him you got into my bed in the morning to play before getting up and asked whether he ever got into mummy's bed to play with her...

You laughed. How like him to talk to others about you and say nothing to your face! Ah well, you'd always known what to expect... And expecting it, I reciprocated. I suppose that's it...

Yes, she replied. He could be so terribly abrupt, so very frightening. When he corrected her English he did it so sharply that she thought she'd better not open her mouth again. It was obvious that he couldn't think himself into a child's world; if something annoyed him he just let go. One day, in a tone that terrified her, he said, Don't you dare teach my child to bow and click his heels like a German when he says good morning... It came as a surprise to Ilse because normally he seemed little concerned about your upbringing, gave her no instructions and made no comments on your behaviour. But perhaps, she thought now, the norms were there without her even being aware of them.

—The bringing up of a gentleman?

Yes. But that wasn't my concern. It had nothing to do with me – that was your parents' affair. I had to see you were fed and looked after, not to influence or teach you anything.

Presumably most fathers of this class had acted in much the same way, you put in.

Very much so, she replied. The children were left to their nannies and the parents had little to do with them. Their upbringing as gentlemen must come later, through schooling, she thought.

—The confirmation, I'd say. He had his ways of trying to make me into the sort of son he wanted long before I went to school . . . She must remember the morning when, exploding with rage, he rushed to get my mother's curlers to put in my hair which was as shamefully long as a girl's. No? Or that other day when, in imitation of the Aldershot tattoo finale, rehearsed for hours with tin soldiers, I turned on the gramophone concealed under the table and the first strains of God Save the King were heard. Immediately, above the music, came a stentorian command: Stand up! Stand to atttention! Humbly I crept out to do my duty. When the record at last expired, he insisted again: Always stand to attention when the national anthem is played . . . And, turning to leave, confided in a loud voice to my mother: He's got all the makings of a soldier, you'll see . . .

No, I don't remember. You never told me, you were so quiet about things that sometimes I feel now I didn't pay enough attention to your feelings . . .

—Mmm . . . Well, all children went through things of the sort, you commented, things which left scars barely visible to others but which the child never forgot. More interesting were the things you couldn't remember, had perhaps repressed, the invisible scars as it were. Blankness – the blankness between the distance and closeness of your mother – revealed more important, forgotten scars, possibly. Because, on the one hand she was like a distant goddess who could work miracles while, on the other, she was paradoxically powerless to change those steps that lay, like granite, before you on the ascent to adulthood. What lay in that blankness, Ilse?

Blankness, Ronnie? I would say that she didn't have much to do with you when you were small. Life offered them such a lot, didn't it? I mean, they were always in a hurry to go riding or play tennis or to rush off to parties. From shortly after your birth your mother was at home little more than for meals. Sometimes she and her mother would come in and the baroness would say, Isn't he sweet? . . . but neither of them picked you up and carried you round. Even at the Manor I don't remember your mother kissing you, there was no physical contact . . .

—No touch. It's frightening how the English fear touching each other. And she wasn't English even. Do you think she resented having a child so young?

She never showed it, but perhaps she felt you had come too soon because she had been married only a year when you were born. I always felt that she was much too young to be a mother . . . But after Colin was born she grew much closer to you. I told her then that she ought to give you more of her attention, and she did, she really made herself because she was someone who could do what was necessary. She taught you to ride, do you remember? Round and round the paddock on the pony. You hated it. It was one of those things that you had to do – you were that sort of family, that was your world – a world that I thought was fantastic at the time . . .

Not that Ilse had known then that you hated riding, you'd never told her. It gave her such a pang when she learned from your mother later. How terrible to feel so close to a child and not to know what you were feeling! But then you never complained. There wasn't anything I expected from you that you didn't do. It was rather sad, really, that there was never an opportunity to praise you . . .

Restlessly, almost relentlessly, you quarried their memories for an image of your mother. Doris, the nursery maid, remembered that she always came in at bath-time to see to you, and you had a whale of a time, splashing and larking about with her. But otherwise there wasn't much contact; it was Ilse who had complete control . . . Your mother was such a sweet person, I expect she thought Ilse could control you and she could love and enjoy you. Even in the dining room when your parents were there it was Ilse who'd correct you. She was starchy, severe, as I've said, but that didn't hurt you, did it?

No, surely not, you replied. But wasn't she implying that, because of Ilse, your mother played only part of the normal parental role . . .

Yes, parents with nannies don't have an intimate relationship with their children. That's something the likes of us don't know because we've always had our parents round to tell us what to do. I'd sooner have our way of living, to tell the truth. Parents in your class of family don't enjoy the child as parents should, and the children can't enjoy the parents' companionship because there isn't any. I don't mean that your mother didn't love you, because she did, you know . . .

—Always coming and going, though, wasn't she? Still, there must have been other times that she spent with me.

Riding she did with you, didn't she? I remember, whenever she called, a slight scowl would come over your face. You didn't want to go, I don't know why, you just weren't keen.

—You knew that then? Ilse didn't, and she was much closer to me.

Oh yes, I could see it straight away. That was the only thing. Otherwise you seemed a happy, open child. You were never underhand – you couldn't get away with it because your face gave you away. You're very like your mother, aren't you? After you left last time, I said to my husband, my God, he's the image of his mother! And you are . . . She was a lovely woman, you know, she idolized you. You could see that by the way she was always happy and smiling when she was with you. Charming to everyone, including me and I was the lowliest of the low . . .

Only once had she said something to Doris that angered her. As Doris was coming out of the butler's pantry one day you came running noisily through and she shouted, Ronnie, stop rushing about . . . Your mother happened to be at the top of the stairs. She came down and said, It's *master* Ronnie to you. You must call both the children master . . . Doris was upset at being told off: why should she have to address a little boy, even a baby who couldn't understand, by this term? Ilse didn't. It made Doris feel rebellious and she would only say it when your mother was about. But she knew, too, that it represented an inescapable fact . . .

You were being groomed to be a gentleman when you grew up. Do you know what I mean? – groomed for your class of people. Everything seemed concentrated round that. Whereas we were brought up with the knowledge that one day we would have to go out to work to earn our living, you were brought up to think that even if one day you had to do something it was more important to be a young gentleman. What do I mean by that? A toff, educated, someone superior – not just you, I don't mean, but the others too. In fact, you were there when your mother told me off. Whether it registered or not I don't know. But one couldn't escape it, one was aware of it all the time. I was the little maid of the house –

—And I was the little master . . . A being of innate superiority who, for no certain reason (you wrote in the interview diary), felt condemned to an equally profound sense of nullity. The former came as a fact from the world; the latter was an innate flaw that gnawed at the vitals of a superiority which derived simply, as Doris saw, from being. (Bert, you reflected, couldn't simply be; he had to *do* in order to be the gardener he was. A gentleman's essence, on the other hand, required no doing to confirm its being – an ontological scandal, if ever there was.) But this innate right which others of your class so mysteriously enjoyed, so concretely incarnated, passed you by. And they saw it . . .

You were always on the defensive, always looked as if you were ready for what was going to come, Mrs Carvell recalled. Deep down it seemed you were frightened of something . . .

Carvell agreed. You were always nervous, thinking twice before doing anything. Especially out riding. It was the first pony that had done it, he thought. They'd been told it had been hunted but no sooner did it hear the huntsman's horn than it started to paw the ground, neigh and lunge with all four feet off the ground. It was all Carvell could do to hang onto it and to you. Your father shouted at him to hold the pony. Carvell replied that he'd better take you home . . . No, keep them both out, your father said in his abrupt sort of way, it'll do them both good . . . He sounded as though he didn't care two hoots, he never had any patience teaching you to ride, he'd just shout instead. When Carvell told him you didn't seem keen, he answered shortly, Well, he'll have to get used to it . . .

Your mother showed much more patience, she wanted you to enjoy hunting. When there was a meet locally, Carvell would lead the pony and her horse, Bert would drive you, your mother and Ilse out, and then Bert and Ilse would follow the hounds by car so as to pick you up soon after mid-day. Then Carvell would hack back with the pony so that you didn't have to ride home.

—It needed a nanny, a gardener and a groom to take a child out hunting, you mean?

That was the usual thing in those days, yes. I was disappointed that you didn't enjoy riding because there would be no one to carry on when your father no longer wanted to hunt. But you always seemed glad to get off the pony, and your mother would often leave hunting early in the afternoon to get home in time to read to you . . .

And not only in the afternoons, Mrs Carvell put in. She'd give up a day's hunting to bring you back sometimes. She always protected you when your father had one of his outbursts, didn't she, William? She had to pour oil on troubled waters. She didn't want to be annoyed with him but it was you she always covered for. You were the apple of her eye and that caused antagonism between your father and her. As soon as you started to cry – which you used to do very often out riding – it was, poor darling! And the poor darling knew quite a bit, unless you cried and made a scene your mother wouldn't rescue you. Out riding, where she had you to her-self, she could show her love without fear of rebuke from Ilse, you see. She worshipped you, she really did. I'm surprised she ever got married again, I'd have said that if she just had you . . . Mrs Carvell laughed.

—A spoiled child, then . . .

You knew how much she loved you and you played up to it. Now, for myself, I wouldn't let my son know how much I cared for him, I've never let William see I feel sorry for him when he's ill because he'd play on it. I've no patience with people who are in any way neurotic . . .

You said nothing, waiting for her to continue. After a pause, she added: All the same, however much your mother and Ilse loved you, you still lacked something that only parents can give. My son had far more from me than you ever had given to you – not financially, but bodily and mentally. And I had the housework and cooking to do as well. A nanny is a barrier, always a barrier . . .

Perhaps, she went on, things might have been different if Ilse had been an ordinary English nanny who had time for the nice side of mothering, the being together and playing with a child. But she was too busy cleaning for that. As a result you were left to amuse yourself with Dolcie, Mrs Winteringham's spastic daughter. When Mrs Carvell told Ilse she wouldn't let a child of hers play with a woman who was not only mentally deficient but potentially dangerous, Ilse didn't reply . . . She was quite happy really to leave you with Dolcie so she could get on with her cleaning. You can't have had much of a time with her for a playmate, can you, though?

—Oh! . . . Poor old Dolcie, infant-adult companion of loneliness, expiatory slave, object of fear and curiosity! You had only to look at her heavy, Beethoven-like face to know she wasn't right in the head. Lamely stomping across the yard clutching her belly she'd mutter, I'm going to have a little calf soon, to explain (it later seemed) the period pains which wracked her desire for something of her own to mother. A new-born chick was quite safe in her clumsy hands – the same hands which took a knife to her own mother, Mrs Winteringham – and which, with untold strength, could lift fallen tree trunks in the playground. Sometimes she frothed at the mouth, her eyes rolled in their yellowish whites and she went for you with a stick in her hand. Deliberately, you provoked her anger, knowing that she was too slow and uncoordinated to get you; deliberately, too, though it needed no provocation, you got her to squat down and pee in the shrubs in order to examine her. No one ever knew, or if they did they didn't care. Poor old Dolcie! Some fire burned in her mind, burned through her raucously repeated sound – Watch out, tonight is bonfire night! – and finally consumed her in the mental asylum to which, unable to cope any longer, her mother consigned her . . .

—Poor old Dolcie!

Yes, Eileen agreed, but it was her mother she really pitied. And that was what your mother must have felt because she never excluded Dolcie. Eileen would have thought twice about letting a child of hers play with Dolcie – but your mother was so sweet-natured that she would never have shut anyone out. The pity was that you didn't have anybody else to play with, only when other children came to tea or you went to their house. Otherwise you spent hours in the garden or indoors on your own . . .

Watching, following Bert on each of his tasks, from manure heap to hot-house by way of the tool-shed, watching seeds being sown and wood being chopped, the earth being turned and the sewer pumped out, loam being crumbled between hard, calloused fingers and peach blossoms pollinated with a rabbit's-tail stick; hearing him talk about the darts team he ran and beer at the pub and the visit of someone in a white robe called Ghandi and the progress of war in somewhere called Spain . . . And we'll soon have our lot, too, you mark my word . . . Watching, following, you felt free to let yourself go, ramble along the way you felt best, seeing the two notes pass from white hands to calloused every Saturday noon, when he touched his hat and later on said, twenty-five bob for the missus and five for me, we'll have a pint tonight seeing as how Saturday only comes once a week . . . Feeling there was something good in sowing seeds that later became plants with funny names like kohlrabi, celeriac and shallot, marshalled in lines across freshly hoed earth; feeling that here was a result one could touch, and even more strongly that this was a job which had to be done, that could never be said to be gratuitous, as shooting and fishing and hunting so obviously seemed. Bert's work had a useful purpose, was contained in the seed he sowed, and everything had a reason that could clearly be seen, unlike the rest of the world that dictated the course of childhood. With Bert I felt free . . .

Well, I had more to do with you, telling you things, than ever your father and mother did. Or Ilse. The majority of the time you were with me, it was more of a life for a boy up in my old house than down there in your big house, happier altogether. There was no home life for you like there is in the poor class. There may be no brass, but they do get a family life with their parents. You never had that . . .

Knowing that he enjoyed his employers' confidence as long as they let their son spend so much time with him, Bert would act the fool, tell jokes and tales and little kiddie things like putting your hat on back to front to make you laugh. I'm daft like that, still am, you know, because I've always liked kiddies. And you were very interesting because you talked nice, were brought up to know right from wrong, took notice when an adult spoke to you. By the hour you stood watching me at work, asking all sorts of things . . .

—Just watching?

Yes. You never said anything about doing things. You was frightened to touch anything, frightened to get your hands dirty. If you did – straight away old Ilse would say, You've got dirty hands, go in and wash. She didn't let you have your head as a boy – bugger about with the others when they came. They'd get up to mischief, swing on the shrubs and pull them about, and you wouldn't. You'd stand on the lawn and watch. You wasn't told not to go with them, it was automatic, you knew you hadn't to go in there. You lost a lot of pranks, wasn't allowed to go out and have the fun we did as kids . . .

—No . . .

Well, you weren't allowed to mix with many other children, were you? Only those of your class. It was a very isolated life you lived. Whereas for us working-class children life was much freer, Doris recalled . . . Out on the common, climbing trees, paddling, making houses by the Birches, dirt-tracking on bikes round the footpaths – free from morning till tea-time in summer, boys and girls together. And in winter there was the thing she enjoyed above all else: hunting . . . As soon as we heard the hounds, mum would leave off the washing and we'd jump on our bikes. Almost everyone in the village loved to follow the hounds. As soon as they saw a fox they'd stand and holler, and the huntsmen would gallop up. Which way did he go? . . . Across there . . . And then the gentry and their children would gallop over the fields, we loved to watch them. Of course, it was them and us, but that didn't matter, we had a marvellous time of it. Often mum and I got home just in time to finish the washing before it got dark . . .

One thing she didn't like, though, was to see the fox killed. Once they ran a fox to ground in front of her. She watched as the huntsmen put the Jack Russell terriers down and then as they brought the fox up dead. The huntsmen cut off the brush and wanted to blood her. She turned and ran. Fancy wanting to put fox's blood on my face, it was horrible . . .

—You've just reminded me . . . Silently, inexplicably, Carvell led the pony across a foggy field towards a dell. Under the trees hounds were milling about, snarling and yapping. Riders on horses and others on foot, amongst them a man in a red coat, watched as the hounds pulled bits of meat about between them. The man in the red coat took a bit from one of them, stuck his fingers in it and rubbed the blood on your cheeks and forehead. The smell was repulsive, but worse was not knowing which part of the fox the bloody meat came from. No one explained, it was jut another of those mysteries of childhood. But when people began to offer their congratulations, a twinge of fearful pleasure filled the inner void, if only momentarily, bloodily, with the satisfaction of becoming one of the elect. Another of those steps that lay frighteningly immutable on the path through childhood had been overcome. The blood caked and your cheeks itched. Ilse was horrified yet proud and didn't insist that you wash immediately. That evening there was a knock on the bedroom door and the huntsman, looking extraordinarily ordinary in sports coat and flannels, approached the bed with a brown paper bag. You sat up in surprise and he opened the bag to show you the grinning fox's head and the tail which he had brought as an additional sign of election. Bloodstained, they were less frightening than the human rituals which had accompanied their dissection that morning; and you accepted them as of right (in proof of which, suitably mounted with engraved silver plaques to celebrate the date, mask and brush thereafter hung on the nursery wall) and gravely thanked the huntsman, who was offered five shillings for his trouble by your father downstairs . . .

In the smoking room where, as always, behind his glittering pince-nez, he sat unsmiling in the same armchair, the white wall of the Times *raised in front of and containing him impermeably, a monolithic presence, without likeness to the shrunken old man slumped staring at the wall in a chair by the narrow bed . . .*

Morning, Alexander.

Ah! Old boy.

Did you have a good night? Sleep all right?

I don't know. My memory has gone, hasn't it?

Yes.

Everything's gone really. I've never felt so depressed.

I'm sorry. I know it's hard.

He looks out of the window. Those people out there don't do the things any more . . . I have nobody who comes and asks me to share a day's shooting.

No. Well, those were other times.

I haven't got a single thing that anybody needs me for . . .

No. But there are other things you can still do.

Look at that there. He lifts his eyes to the wardrobe. I haven't looked in it, no one tells me to, they don't say, close that window thing, it's just there . . .

I know what it's like to be depressed. But it's possible to work your way through it and come out stronger.

If only it could all end peaceably. I'm finished, I want to die . . .

Now don't say that. You've got things to live for still.

All the things that meant anything no longer exist. Shooting an occasional pheasant, a partridge. Do you get any shooting, old boy? No. You're not always idle, are you?

Not exactly.

Ah! I'm a negative quantity. I wish I could just pop off quietly. The tears start to run down his cheeks.

I understand. Death seems like a release. I'm sorry we haven't talked about it before. But then, we've never talked, really, about ourselves, have we?

I don't know, old boy. He pulls out a handkerchief.

Do you remember when I was young, at Amnersfield? With Janey, Ilse, William Carvell? You had a good life then, you're rounding off that life now.

Yes? The war came between us, didn't it?

Perhaps . . . I was thinking this morning of that green chair you used to sit in, when Ilse brought me in I stroked the arm to

see the nap change from jade to emerald. I tried to show you—
Ilse?
No, you.
She looked after you, didn't she?
Yes. Brought me up, I suppose. Perhaps that's why we've
never talked.
He blows his nose, returns the handkerchief to his cuff. His
hands wander in search of something, find the stick hanging
on the arm of the chair and grasp it with unexpected firm-
ness . . . I'm pleased to take part in this conversation with you,
old man, but I have to tell you that it is doing nothing to allevi-
ate my state of mind . . .
I'm sorry . . . For a time we sit in silence. Well, another time
when you're less low, perhaps. I have to go now, it's a long
drive to London.
Ah!
I'll be back very soon. Take care of yourself . . .
He looks up; through the horn-rimmed glasses which have
out-grown his face the watery gaze reflects, apprehensively, a
common fate.

—No one could have known me better than you. In many senses you
brought me up. Can you give me some idea, finally, of how I seemed to you?

You were an easily worked out, well-behaved child, Ronnie. You never
refused to do anything I wanted, never complained. Even when you were
in turmoil, you didn't reveal your feelings, never sought consolation.
Sometimes I now feel that I didn't try hard enough to understand what you
were feeling. But it seemed to me that that was your nature.

—I'm struck by the passivity of it.

Maybe it was contentedness, although it's true, you weren't as inven-
tive as other children. When John Walker came to tea, you seemed happy
to stand and watch him climb every tree in the garden. Often I felt it would
be nice if you were more adventurous, but I cared for you too much to be
critical. A lot of the time you were in the garden with Bert. He found time
for you as no one else did. He was someone who listened to you, he
brought you out, although sometimes I felt that he went a bit too far and

ought to have considered you more as the son of the house. I may even have said something to him about it once or twice . . .

—But there was Dolcie, too. Didn't it seem strange that I was allowed to play with her?

No. She was like a child, simple but good-natured.

—She took a knife to her mother once . . .

Oh, she would never have done anything like that to you. Perhaps with her parents, because people do do things to their parents, don't they? We sometimes went to tea with them and Dolcie always behaved all right . . .

All the same, Ilse reflected, she should have been more aware of your need for children of your own age to play with. Until these past weeks of conversation, she had simply accepted the fact that you weren't allowed to play with the village children, hadn't even thought about it. If she had suggested it to your mother perhaps she wouldn't have minded. Or would she have thought, Oh, if these village children come in the house they'll bring illnesses or habits that you might pick up. Once in touch with another class it might have given you strange feelings and interfered with your upbringing which had to follow a pattern.

You laughed; it would have been a good thing . . .

Maybe, she agreed, but it had nothing to do with her. I had to remember always that you were your parents' child. I couldn't say and do whatever I thought right, it would have caused friction . . .

—That must have been a very difficult position . . .

Yes, it was. And it became harder as time went on and I felt myself becoming increasingly less important in your life. I had always known this would happen, but it was heart-breaking all the same. I'm not sure the hurt can ever be totally overcome. In some ways Colin's birth helped compensate for the loss.

Surely, then, you suggested, she must have regretted not having children of her own.

No, she regretted not having married and set up a home of her own. Things hadn't turned out as they might. At nineteen she had a relationship with a man twenty years older than she – her step-sister's brother-in-law. He and his wife, who were childless, had taken Ilse into their home more or less as their daughter. He fell in love with her, they slept together and then, torn between guilt and love, she tried to free herself. Each time she did her lover fell desperately ill, for he had lost a lung in the first World War. After three years, his wife found a letter he had written to Ilse from abroad and was outraged; Ilse was forced to leave. Although they saw each other infrequently after that, the relationship continued. It was a wrench but also a relief when she came to England. Not long after, she received a letter from her father, who knew nothing of the relationship, in which he mentioned, in passing, that Herr so-and-so had just died.

It was terrible. I never believed the expression about knocking your head against a wall, but that's what I did. Then I went down and told your parents I had lost a relative and asked if I could go home. It was December 9, your birthday, and your mother said I could go for a week. Your father came and comforted me, gave me a drink. Your mother never referred to it. I had said enough for her to guess, and perhaps she was shocked that I was in love with a married man. I got over my grief before long but I have never forgotten the relationship. It's a satisfaction in my life that, once at least, I experienced love, in spite of all the sadness it brought me.

—I'm happy and sad for you at the same time. I'd often wondered whether you could have been happy at the Manor without an emotional relationship . . .

As long as I was with children I was happy. In a sense you filled my life. You were always with me, I was there for you. We slept in the same bedroom until your brother was born, when we went out you always held my hand. You were unhappy on my afternoons off, I know because you made a great effort to appear cheerful. When I went on holiday you missed me very much. Do you remember? I may not have taken it as seriously as I ought . . .

—Ah well! . . . Overall, the image you give is one of dependency, extreme docility. It was my natural character, you think, evident from birth . . .

Yes, so it seemed to me. You were a quiet, uncomplaining baby. You know that I began work with your mother a few days before her confinement and went with the baroness to the nursing home to fetch you and her home. I cared for you almost alone from the beginning . . . For a short time, your mother breast-fed, Ilse recalled, and then, for reasons she was unaware of, gave up. Perhaps your father complained about being disturbed. Ilse took over bottle-feeding; she believed in regular feeding times and if you cried she pushed the pram to the front of the flat to spare your parents. It was the same with nappies, she changed them by schedule. She didn't want you getting used to being clean all the time and making a fuss if you weren't. Your mother protested once about a wet nappy and Ilse replied, He'll have a clean nappy when it's his time . . . It came from her institutional training, she thought, for today she wouldn't keep a baby in dirty nappies, although she would still clock-feed.

Each morning, as soon as she could, she pushed the pram to the fields and woods on the outskirts of Hamburg where no one else went. She hated being with other nannies who sat like hens with their chicks, gossiping. Much of the time was spent with the pram outdoors and by six months you were as brown as a berry. When she put you down, you either lay sucking your thumb or fell asleep. Before you were two you lay in bed in the morning waiting for her to pick you up.

She was well content with you and the job, her first as a children's nurse in private service. She had always wanted to look after children, and only her mother's straitened circumstances after the first World War, the loss of the family bakery and of a number of working-class flats she owned, had forced Ilse to postpone her ambition for seven years and find work as a maid. She was twenty-three when she started her two years' training in an orphanage with 120 babies and infants. A further six months in a maternity home completed her training and confirmed her natural gift for children, leaving her feeling well able to cope in a private home.

In fact, it was lovely, I was on my own, I didn't have people telling me what to do, no longer had to bother about other nurses and whether they liked me or not. Everything was provided and I had a certain comfort. And, of course, I could concentrate all my attention on you.

—Was the orphanage training useful to you in this new situation?

In feeding and cleanliness, yes. Perhaps I concentrated a little more on toilet training than normal. When you were four months old I had you sitting on a pot in a small chair, tied with a nappy, so I could clean the room while I talked to you. Later, I tied you on your pot to the end of the bed until you produced. It was what we did every morning at the orphanage, you see, the only way we could control so many children . . . She laughed. I used to tie you to a laundry pole or a tree in the garden if I had something to do close by. It was my way of training you. Many people think it deprives a child of its freedom and they just let it run around. But I don't think it hurts, do you?

—I wouldn't claim any privilege that an orphan wasn't entitled to, you answered, smiling.

3

We

Sept 3, 1979

'Well,' I said, 'I've been through all the evidence and it confirms what I told you when I first came last month. The house was divided and so was I . . .'

I looked at P. sitting in the chair by the window. His lowered eyes and bowed head, and the light-weight suit that heightened his tan, gave him the appearance of a traveller waiting somnolently for something to happen, I didn't know what. I hastened on:

'A split foreshadowed in my parents, I've come to see. I'd hoped that the evidence would prove that my image of childhood was a fiction − no, a crutch I could at last kick away. Instead . . .'

The airliner banked and the notebook slid from the narrow tray. Through the window the grey water of the reservoirs fell away and the river's gun-metal surface, spanned at Hammersmith, came briefly into view. The ribbons of red houses vanished beneath the cloud and before I had time to collect my thoughts, as intangible as the drifting cloud, I saw through a gap the steel-cold Channel appear.

I picked up the notebook and glanced at the crabbed writing again. How many more pages remained to fill? How many more years? Three and a half with P. had already gone by, recorded in the notebooks which I had brought to read on the flight to Rome. Colin would be waiting at the airport; there was still a part of the past to be filled in.

'What do you hope to find out from him?' P. asked before I left.
'About the war, when everything changed . . .'

P's silence seemed particularly heavy. Perhaps he thought my time would be better spent in the couple of sessions I was going to miss. Reality for him is not out there but inside me. Never mind. I turned the pages again to that almost forgotten September morning in '79 when, after a summer of others' memories, I closed P's double doors behind me to embark on a new search into the past.

'. . . All the same', I went on, 'the interviews with Ilse and the others served a purpose. They showed what was made of me. But that's like looking through a single lens, isn't it? What did I make of their making – that's the part I can't distinguish. Without it I can't write about the past.'

He looked up. 'Perhaps you feel you haven't integrated the past into your life.'

'Oh no!' I protested. 'I've been doing nothing else for the last ten years. As I told you last time, I don't want to live with it any longer. By recreating the past on paper I can dispose of it once and for all. The problem is that the past hasn't left me equipped for the job! . . . ' Schizoid characteristics, a super-ego and id without an ego to balance them – those were the problems, I added. 'How can one write about one's past without an ''I'' as the focus?'

There's a long, almost unbearable silence. I feel as if I've committed a solecism. 'Psychoanalysis, you know,' he says at last, 'doesn't set out to dispose of the past but to understand it. By understanding it one has a choice of how to deal with it. So it's a voyage of discovery we're embarking on . . . ' He pauses. 'I feel, too, that the sort of language you've just been using is jargon. It's your experiences that are important, what you feel and felt in your own words, not some textbook theory . . . '

Another silence.

'What do you want me to talk about then?'

'Whatever comes to your mind.'

His words dispel the last vestiges of thought. I look round the room, trying to gain something from the studied anonymity, muted colours which the light from the half-closed Venetian blinds – ah! we're hidden from view – does nothing to brighten. An antique tallboy and a small, elegant desk beside my chair recall, momentarily, a world beyond these basement walls, beyond the reality of this double-doored dream-box where nothing distracts the gaze. I look at him again but his eyes are lowered. Is he bored? . . .

Sept 6

Today I went straight to the heart of the matter: on the one hand, objectively a member of a privileged class I was, on the other, unable subjectively to fill the role into which I was born. This split, I said, was foreshadowed in my parents. My father incarnated the values of his class and time and, sometimes forcibly, confronted me with them as the only ones open to me; my mother, perhaps because she was American, rejected many of the manifestations of those values and held open the door to possible alternatives. Between the two – the ought and the want – I shuttled uneasily, a traitor to both. 'And to myself,' I added.

While I was speaking I saw an occasional grimace on his face as though to indicate that my words were irrelevant. When I finished he said nothing. Had I talked so long as a form of self-defence?

'I think you're approaching it too much from the top, too theoretically. It'll have to emerge rather from below,' he said.

'Too theoretically? It didn't feel very theoretical living it . . . ' Through the surge of irritation an image arose. I held onto it. 'In the brief moments I spent with my mother as a child in her dressing room she'd pick a ring or bracelet out of her jewel case and tell me stories of far-off places: Colorado, Mexico, Germany . . . '

Enthralled, I sat beside her as she told me about her father, an Irish immigrant cowhand, who used to make the cows stand up so he could warm his bare feet on the grass where they'd been lying. In Colorado, he discovered a silver mine, she said, and made a fortune which he gambled away. Undaunted, he discovered another, became a millionaire and died soon afterwards while she was still a child.

And then there was her mother's father who rode one of the last covered wagons out West. A grocer in Chicago at the time of the great fire in the 1870s, he ran a train of groceries into the city, cornered the market and made a fortune. Shortly after, he fell ill with TB and, on doctor's orders, headed for Denver, the mile-high city, where he founded a prosperous wholesale grocery chain and became a public benefactor whose name is remembered to this day.

'And she'd tell me of her schooldays in California, of meeting Charlie Chaplin, Douglas Fairbanks and Mary Pickford in Hollywood; of the large house in Mexico City where she had lived and where the *peones* assembled in a line on the vast lawn to cut the grass with the serrated tops of sardine tins . . . Her world, it seemed, was not the Manor House, but another, more interesting universe out there. Real life was not here but elsewhere.

For my father, real life was this series of steps I had to climb to adulthood like a pre-determined being . . . Do you understand?'

'Yes.'

'In the evenings sometimes when I was in bed my mother would come in for a moment to say goodnight. She wore long evening dresses that rustled and she came in so lightly that she seemed to float, and there was a scent she wore which remained in the air after she'd gone. She was there only a moment, I can feel myself still reaching out to her as she floated away, unable to stay because . . . because she had to go out to dinner or something. There was an intimacy but also a distance between us. I remember her most as a miracle-worker . . . '

I know, as I say it, that this is grist for his mill, not mine. Indeed, his eyes light up, it's the first time I've seen him in any way animated. 'A miracle-worker! What do you mean?'

I try to explain. She was distant, not apparently involved in my everyday life, but at the same time she could get me out of things I didn't want to do, those things that people of my class had to do. 'She was a potential ally on the path of escape. She might come to the rescue, but on the other hand she might not. She had to be prayed to . . . '

'A tantalizing wizard, perhaps?'

'I suppose so.' I don't like his expression. 'All the people at the Manor talk of her obvious love for me – Mrs Carvell says, with a touch of sardonic exaggeration no doubt, that she wonders that my mother ever married again – but it's not how I lived it. I don't remember her playing with me as one does with a child, getting down to my level. I don't think she could put herself into a child's shoes . . . '

A feeling of sudden anxiety makes me stop. I look at him, knowing already the infallible time-piece he carries in his head. 'I fear you're about to tell me it's time and I'll have to stop.'

'No, there's time. But you're feeling, perhaps, that your mother is about to say that, feeling that you never had enough time with her.'

'That's true. I never did . . . ' I used the brief moments in her dressing room before she went out and I had to return to Ilse to allay my anxieties. Did I have to go away to school? Did I have to go out riding? Couldn't I stay home and play in the garden instead of having to go to dancing class? Would I have to go in the army when I grew up, as my father said? Well, if I didn't, what would I be? She'd shake her head and say I'd have to decide.

' "But how shall I know?" '

' "You'll find out, don't worry, darling. Whatever it is, I hope you'll be happy.'' Happiness was her sole aim. And then she would sigh, as though there were too many questions, and say, ''I wish we could be more like dogs and our children didn't need us for more than a few months. Wouldn't you like that, too?''

' ''Is it true that I wouldn't recognize you as my mother after a year?'' I asked. I don't remember what she said to that. I knew she loved her dogs – but I never forgot the remark.'

I felt him looking at me. 'You just said your mother shouldn't have had children. Why?'

'I said that? When?'

'Just now.'

'Really. Oh well, the unconscious speaking. Perhaps I feel she shouldn't have had me. She was too young, too immature, too dominated by her husband. He was thirteen years older than she. Or I shouldn't have had her. We shouldn't have had each other.'

The words were greeted by a silence so profound, so unremitting, that I felt threatened. 'What's the point of all this? It's as though everything I say is worthless.'

'Why is that? Do you feel you have to say only what I will approve?'

'Perhaps. It's like in childhood, there's no dialogue here. If you don't participate you deny my existence.'

'It shows another side of your mother, doesn't it? She's omniscient, a wizard, but she won't listen to you . . . ' A pause and then: 'It's time . . . '

I get up, thank him and leave feeling dispirited.

Sept 21

Two barren weeks, reporting little incidents that add up to nothing. Where is the totality I aspire to?

His silences still worry me. 'I feel I'm not producing what is required, what you need to push this thing forward.'

'Are you here for me or for yourself?' he asks.

'I wonder sometimes.'

More than once he has suggested that I use the couch. 'It might be easier to get in touch with your childhood.'

'Some other time.' I can't face the cartoon image of analyst and analysand, the supine dependency. I like to see his face, want to keep his silences at bay. During the last session I felt, however, that I was watching his reactions as a means of sensing his approval; the dependency was greater sitting looking at him than lying down, and so I made the move. The couch had no immediate effect; the only image which floated up was of a heavy paving stone, warm brown in colour, well-worked and smooth on top, unhewn beneath. A foundation stone, I thought, the conscious bottom of myself.

Oct 1, 1979

The stone remains immovable. 'The trouble is, you see, that I free-associate when I'm alone, not here with you . . . '

'. . . '

'I thought of that because yesterday, walking across the Heath, an image arose, an image of a star as brilliant as Venus in the evening sky, sparkling enticingly, circling a moon which was full, white and close . . . '

'The moon pale, the star bright?'

'Yes. The moon is cold. I don't ascribe any mythological significance to it. It shines constantly but with a glacial light. The star moves round it like a satellite, like that memory of my mother sweeping in in evening dress to say goodnight.'

'And the moon?'

'Ilse, of course. The reality of day-to-day life, of doing and having to do.'

He asks about Ilse, her age, etc. I recall her white uniform, the super-cleanliness which seemed not to allow her time to play, her pot-training learned at the orphanage. In my mind's eye I see her black hair swept back tight over her head, her brown eyes which miss so little. 'Despite all that, I was happy with her, she gave me a comfort and security I've never forgotten. When I went to interview her, after a time I fell into a sort of hypnotic trance, like a child finding comfort in a mother's voice . . . '

As I said it, I realized that I simultaneously longed for and hated the hypnotic passivity I'd recalled. 'I was her job. But her job was not me, it was a function of a pre-determined future. For all that, she did the job with much love and affection. I never thought it possible that she would invalidate me.' As an afterthought, I added: 'As long as I didn't invalidate her.'

'What do you mean?'

'I don't know . . . Well, as long as I was the child she wanted . . . ' I relate Mrs Carvell's account of Ilse's determination to make a little gentleman of me and her comment that she didn't know what constituted one.

He laughed. It was the first time and I was quite pleased.

'I should have brought you the transcript and you could have seen for yourself.'

'I don't quite understand,' he said, reverting to his usual modulated tone, 'why you are so concerned with someone else's testimony.'

'It's the discovery of myself from outside and for that reason has additional weight. Isn't it of interest to you to know whether this or that happened?'

'Of course . . . '

'But not essential?'

'Not really. It's what you feel that matters, isn't it? I heard a historian who is also an analyst say the other day that all history is today's history since it reflects the preoccupation of a historian writing now . . . '

'Mmm . . . What happens today, in this room, won't have changed tomorrow when today has become the past, will it? What changes are our concerns and thus the questions we ask of the past. But psychoanalysis isn't history, it seems. What actually happened is less important than what is felt to have happened. Is that right?'

'I'd say so, yes.'

'Well then, it doesn't matter what Ilse did or didn't do,' I say bitterly. Silence.

'For her I was only valid if I was a good little boy. Passive, I have to confirm her – her confidence and love – by being what she needed me to be. Not what I was. Only out of her sight, alone in the garden, was I free to be myself.'

Still he says nothing.

'Don't you understand? Everything I really felt was me I had to hide. Even in the garden I knew she might be watching from somewhere. She'd send me out to play but I had to keep clean . . . There's a schizoid thing for you! Play in the dirt but don't get dirty . . . '

'Uh-huh . . . '

There's a long silence. Deep inside myself I see a black hole and I know I have to protect it from Ilse's cleansing hands. She can reach right down in me. But she mustn't find this real me, it's all I have left – and yet I don't want it, it's inadmissible, black, guilty . . .

'Yes. And it's to recognize this side of yourself that's the aim of analysis,' he says . . .

I looked out of the plane window at the brilliant blue sky and white, snow-like clouds; from below nothing ever had the same elemental clarity. Over the intercom the captain's voice announced that we were just passing Paris, invisible to our left. I tried to recall, after so many years of flying to Spain, when last I had flown this route to the south. The years unreeled in vain and then it came to me. I pulled the map out of the pocket in the seat and checked. Yes – once before, in the private plane Janey and Teddy Leroy, her airman lover, hired to fly us away, early one summer morning, from Amnersfield without a hint that we would never return. The de Havilland Rapide seemed a part, nothing more, of the continuing adventure of war, and Colin and I climbed in excitedly. The pilot left the cabin door open and we watched him at the controls and then, in mid-air, reading a map without apparently looking where we were flying; he had only four fingers remaining on both hands. We landed at le Bourget, a half-way point, and drove into Paris for lunch. It was the first year after the war . . .

I leafed through another of the notebooks; that flight, of course, was where the book would have to end, I thought – the book I had been unable to write for ten years.

March 2, 1980

Behind closed lids, an unformulated image haunts me; the image of a bundle, curved or bowed, with something or someone next to it on the left. A person: Ilse? Is the bundle me, bowed? *Doblegado*. Everything is totally motionless, almost lifeless. Are the indentations in the blanket cords hidden by the material? Ilse watching a silent bundle, intenseness mingled with pride in her eyes. Don't move: her pride is my stillness, silence. The curvature of the bundle is the slight protrusion of stomach and hips; feet and head are pressed down flat, hidden from view. Don't move and everything will be all right. If I retreat into myself, lie absolutely still, she will go away. I vanish to make her vanish. She and I are two stillnesses, silences – waiting. She will go and I'll stay. And when she goes I can move . . .

'Where to?' he asks.

'To my mother,' I answer. 'I can't go while Ilse is there. She says, "you mustn't bother mummy now. Mummy is busy, mummy is talking to daddy, mummy is getting ready to go out." I don't know if it really happened, but it feels like it.'

'She doesn't let you have as much of your mother as you want . . .'

'Ah!' Out of the darkness surges a need to hold my mother; a bond, the warmth of an embrace. Since her death I have hardly thought of her. 'I mustn't tell Ilse I love my mother for fear I may lose her, Ilse . . . Does that make sense?'

'Yes. They may have been jealous of each other's relationship with you.'

In the silence I feel, with a weight I can hardly describe, Ilse's silent, stubborn disapproval of something – clothes, a toy – my mother has bought. Rock-like, immutable, sure of herself, Ilse stands there in silent disapproval. I want my mother, yet I fear to side with her lest I anger Ilse . . .

'What's it mean,' I ask, 'to be looked after by someone who isn't your mother while your mother is actually there?'

Silence. I realize it's an impossible question.

'Having two mothers, I suppose,' he says at last.

The words strike me with great force. 'Two mothers! Split between each, neither sufficient in herself. Why have I never seen this? . . .' Ilse, surrogate but operative mother; my mother, the actual but inoperative mother; Ilse in constant and exclusive attendance; my mother, coming and going – the distant star and the cold, close moon . . . 'Two mothers and I'm torn between them . . .'

'The caring and the tantalizing mothers. And you split them – into the good and the bad mother.'

'Oh!' There's a long silence. 'I split them! Not they me . . .' So many contradictory feelings surge through me that I can't put them into words for him. Finally, as though to neutralize the confusion, I ask: 'Does a child normally feel that its mother is both good and bad?'

'Certainly. All mothers have to be frustrating as well as loving. But being consoled by another mother who seems unfrustrating makes it harder to reconcile the two . . .'

'Yes,' I say; but I'm not certain I understand. It seems outside my field of experience. 'It's important, I suppose, to reconcile the two.'

'Crucial,' he says with unexpected firmness. 'All children have to reconcile contradictory feelings, love and hatred, of their mother. But it was made harder because you could split the two . . .'

'Oh Christ! Is that why I can't make good the split in myself?'

'Well, it makes it harder, I'm sure.'

His tone is so neutral that I feel myself a specimen swept along in a flood tide. I grab at a passing branch. 'It's not as simple as that. They both loved me, they were both good. But the one tied me down and the other refused to release me.' I feel angrily triumphant as I hang onto my raft.

'You've never forgiven your mother for leaving you with Ilse, have you?'

'No! I've never forgiven her for not being the kind of mother I wanted – an island in the sea from which a child can set sail on its own, always sure there's a refuge to return to.'

'In her social situation she didn't have to be more than a part-time mother. Ilse gave you the constancy you yearned for,' he says mildly.

'No! She didn't let me sail into the unknown. She kept me tied to her. I know, I know, this business of being tied to the pot is so classically Freudian that I can't take it seriously myself.'

'Well, it's a screen memory which can represent many things.'

'It's not a memory at all. I didn't know about it until I interviewed Ilse . . .' A tightness like a band of iron encloses my head and with it the bundle image returns – but now without the stillness. Ilse seems to have gone. I can move, one of the cords is undone; but instead of moving, I am overwhelmed with panic. Ilse will think I've undone the bond deliberately. I am even less able to move than when tied . . .

My words are met with silence.

'I'm there not knowing what to do,' I continue. 'Torn . . . Shall I assert my freedom? If I do, it'll be seen as an act of defiance and I'll be tied up again. If I don't . . . Yes, I can accept being bound, accept not being bound; what's intolerable is not being bound when I'm supposed to be.'

He has vanished somewhere. Why?

'I wish you'd say something.'

'To tie you down with words?'

'No. I want to know if this is the right track, want consolation.'

'You need the security of being bound.'

'You can't imagine . . .' Tears of frustration begin to form behind my lids. 'It's deep inside, this wanting, needing to be bound . . . Needing, wanting to be free . . . Is there anything more splitting?'

'Uh-huh . . .'

'What does that mean? Yes?'

Long pause. 'Something like that . . .'

I laugh bitterly; he likes his manipulative little practices. But I stay with the image despite him. 'Yes – I might as well get up, that's it, I want to get up, take the pot and fling the whole lot at her. I want to get up now and leave this room and have done with the whole thing.'

'Why don't you?'

'Why don't I? Yes, why don't I? Because I know that in half an hour I'll think it was irrational.'

'You're frightened that I'll punish you.'

'Yes. No. I don't know . . . I think I needed to feel bound to be secure. Can you see that? I chose it. Security, my God!'

'The security of a prison . . .'

'That's it, exactly.' With the words comes the image of a prisoner, not myself, seeing the door of his cell ajar, the main gates inadvertently open and beyond – freedom. He can escape if he acts resolutely, spontaneously. He hesitates, thinks, what is the best course? Indecision paralyses him. The known security against the tempting uncertain freedom. 'You know, I always thought that Ilse tying me to the bed was something ludicrous, funny.'

'It wasn't funny then,' he says softly.

'No. It's despairing to need a prison. Why didn't I defy her?'

'The strength of a woman who ties you to a bed can hardly be challenged openly by a child...'

'You could always try. I didn't, I needed Ilse, her security and love. I couldn't leave her because I was frightened that my mother wouldn't be there to replace her. I think that's it... Yes, it was my choice. The role of little prisoner was more profitable than the alternative. As long as I was good, did what they wanted, the more they might let me do what I wanted. It was a way to freedom – freedom from, not freedom to...'

'Uh-huh.' There's a long silence and then he says quietly, 'It's time...'

As I get up time suddenly reassembles as present. I am a man, nearly fifty, where a minute ago I was a child.

March 7

Sitting outside his house, I wait for the patient to leave. I don't want to be seen, perhaps. It's night, and in the dark of the car, looking at the lighted Venetian blinds, I begin to sense something sinister. It's as though I'm waiting to kill someone. I shake myself: these are cinema fantasies of gunmen in darkened cars, I tell myself, as I see the patient, a man much younger than I, leaving. As soon as I have laid myself on the couch, still warm from his presence, I blurt out: 'What a lot of shit must be said in this room!'

'Perhaps you feel that only you should be here. You're jealous of others coming.'

'Really?'... It seems ridiculous. I let the idea settle to see if it roots. No. Meanwhile, the assassination reverie returns to my mind. 'It was you I wanted to kill, I think.'

Silence.

'Maybe I feel you're tying me down. I resent having to come here...'

'Perhaps you're jealous of your brother. The younger patient having my attention.'

'Maybe it's him I want to kill.' Indeed, as I say it, I feel quite murderous towards Colin as a child. It passes, and for a time I say nothing. Then: 'I've just come from re-reading Ilse's transcripts. Her rigid routines made me feel angry. I expect I wanted to kill her at times.'

'Does that surprise you?'

'Yes . . .' More than surprise I feel shaken. In the silence I see myself looking back down at my infanthood, as though through a glass funnel that narrows at the far end and it turns in my hand almost instantly into a dagger. 'I always destroy what I love . . .'

'. . .'

The silence continues until it's almost unbearable. Nothing comes to mind, it's as though I have to hold myself back.

'What are you thinking?'

'Nothing . . .'

'Perhaps there are things you don't want to say.'

'No . . . Yes. I feel I even wanted to kill my mother.'

'. . .'

'I can't believe it.'

'Children very often are frightened of the aggression they feel towards their parents,' he says.

'Yes? How do they get over it?'

'By discovering that their mother isn't destroyed by it, continues to love them.'

'I never discovered this. My rage seemed so destructive that I can't remember ever daring to express it.'

'No memory of even wanting?'

'No, although I must have wanted to.'

'You were frightened that your rage would destroy your mother – the mother you couldn't have enough of.'

As he says it I'm aware of a sensation like shimmering water. 'My mother would dissolve if I expressed hatred of her.'

'. . .'

'Yes, dissolve. I couldn't do it. She would vanish. And then my father would stamp on me and I would dissolve.'

There's a long, anguished silence. Then I say: 'The little I had of her dissolved with my brother's birth. There was nothing left.'

'. . .'

'Nothing. If I couldn't have everything I didn't want anything. Go away, that's what I wanted to say to her. But as soon as I thought it I was frightened. She might go and I would lose her forever. I was torn between the two . . . '

'Your brother was a rival for her affection.'

'Yes . . . His arrival smashed everything, smashed even old Ilse . . . ' I see her now, in a white uniform, coming into the bedroom where, through the window, a late summer sun is shining brightly on the bed where I'm lying, a five-year-old, taking comfort in her presence. She is bringing scones without butter, the hollows filled with honey. I've just had a saline drip to correct the 'acidosis' which began with an attack of vomiting that continued until I was bringing up only fluid. "Your eyes were very hollow and withdrawn, it looked as though you might go any minute," Ilse said. "It was the only time you were really ill. Perhaps you felt a bit excluded. You suffered, I know, when you couldn't sleep in my bedroom any longer because I had to have Colin with me . . . "

'It's one of the rare times that Ilse commented on my feelings.'

'You lost your consoler.'

'What do you mean?'

'When you felt excluded by your mother you could console yourself with Ilse who was entirely yours.'

'To sleep with, you mean?'

' . . . '

'Well, I did, as you know. And then I was kicked out. After that I brought down steel shutters inside myself to keep them all out.'

'And to protect yourself from the pain you felt,' he says.

'I suppose so . . . ' And, as though it were happening again, I retreat to the safety behind the shutters. In the inner darkness faint flickering shadows begin to move, there's a yearning for something – something hidden. From the other side of the door come murmurs, low voices. I numb myself and turn away. 'I can do without them . . . '

There's a silence, and then he says: 'The paradise on the other side of the door which you felt your brother had taken from you. The mother's breast . . . '

'My mother didn't breast-feed,' I reply angrily. 'She gave up after a fortnight with me, according to Ilse. Possibly my father complained about the inconvenience of being woken up.'

He says nothing.

'It made me angry reading that.' Even as I say it I sense not anger but a renewed yearning. 'I never had enough of her, not even as a baby.'

I wait for him but he remains silent.

'Don't you take any account of early infanthood? I thought you were of the object-relations school. Surely it's concerned with the infant's original relationship to its mother. Well, I didn't have one.'

'That sounds a bit theoretical,' he says finally, 'as though you're writing your book.'

'Well, you know I'm not, I haven't got the necessary information yet.'

After another pause, he says: 'Perhaps you're angry because you feel I can't make good the loss of your mother's breast.'

'Well, you can't, can you?'

'Being expelled from the Garden of Eden is part of the human condition, isn't it?

'What does that mean?'

' . . . '

'It's just one of those sayings . . . '

'You wanted more of your mother than you could have, didn't you?'

Again that phrase. What does it mean? 'What did I want that I couldn't have?'

'What most children probably want,' he replies, 'a greater intimacy with their mother than is possible. A mother has to leave, do other things, be with the father, sleep with him.'

'Supposing I didn't have what a child objectively should be entitled to . . . '

'I don't think you were deprived of what you could realistically hope for from your mother.' The answer is sharp, and I don't like it.

'What are you saying then? That I got it wrong?'

' . . . '

'Well?'

'You didn't go through that process of gradual disillusionment, did you? Children learn in day-to-day reality that they can't have as much as they want of their parents.'

'And I never learned? . . . '

'You didn't have that day-to-day reality with your mother. There was the excitement of her flitting in, the disappointment of her flitting out . . . Ilse represented constancy – a restrictive security, in some senses.'

'The two of them, again. None of this helps . . . ' The bitterness wells up. 'I can do without them . . . ' I hear the echo of a child's defiance: I'm all right on my own, I don't need them – and I know that I'm scared.

' . . . '

'Whistling in the dark, hoping that they'll be there. I couldn't do without them – and I still can't. Why else should I spend so much time trying to resurrect them?'

Still he says nothing.
'And why can't I?'
He says something in a voice so low that I ask him to repeat it. I hear him say again: 'Perhaps you want them in order to destroy them in you.' The words are like a blow on the head.
'No! It isn't possible, is it?'
He doesn't reply, and I sink into a bitter silence.

April 10, 1980

I dream very little, or rather I recall very few dreams. I don't like them, I suppose, and so it is always with a slight sense of achievement that I produce one for him. Bert had tried to commit suicide, and was sitting up in bed looking well despite it. ''If I had your father's money I'd have been able to do it properly,'' he says. That was all.
'What do you associate with the dream?'
'Something he said to me once. ''Divorce is only for the rich, the poor can't afford it.'' I even remember where he said it, bent over the sewage pump in the garden trying to get it to work . . . '
'Did he die in the dream?'
'No, he didn't have the means . . . I recall, in my interviews, that he said I was much happier with him in the garden than at home, he believed that the ''poor class'' had much closer family ties than the rich.'
'In your specific case, perhaps,' he puts in.
'Well . . . ' To myself I say the generalization is probably true. At the same time another association with the dream emerges. 'If he had had the means he would have been a father to me . . . '
'In not killing him off, you're perhaps asserting that his model of fatherhood was better than your father's.'
'I wasn't killing him, he was committing suicide.'
'But it's *your* dream . . . '
'Yes, all right . . . He was the only father I really had. He was the only person I felt free with, for whom I didn't have to play a role. Life inside the Manor was like a factory running to an authoritarian discipline, in which cogs pulled me along, conveyor belts pushed me out . . . Oh, I don't know, sometimes I think I've just invented this to justify a sense of alienation. What do you think?'
After a time, he says, 'I think you have a yearning for a father like him.'
'Mmm . . . I've come to believe that sons are better off without fathers. Sartre attributed his lack of deforming super-ego to the fact that his father died young. Do you think that fathers are necessary?'

In the silence I hear the scratchings of some string instrument in the room above. They irritate me; I want to say, Is that thing being tuned or is it one of your children trying to play a tune? But he is already saying: 'How would a child become a man otherwise?'

'It would be a good thing in my view if children didn't become *men* . . . '

'You're speaking of a particular socio-cultural situation . . . '

'The one I live in . . . Is that a cello?'

'I think so,' he replies, and I let it pass. Then he adds: 'Your father hasn't figured much up to the present. Why is that, do you think?'

'Because there was no possibility of a human relationship there. My first memories of him are all threatening . . . ' I recall a number of these, concluding with the moment when he threatened to do up my hair in my mother's curlers because I looked like a girl. 'I knew then that I couldn't fill the role, could never be a man like him. Moreover, I didn't want to be like him and, increasingly, I came to fear that I was like him.'

'And why didn't you want to be like him?'

'That's pretty clear from what I've just said, isn't it? Moreover, he was a failure. That probably accounts for his bitterness. Nowadays, I can feel sorry for him sometimes . . . ' I go on to explain the little I know of his life. The son of an Indian Civil Servant, he was brought up with relatives in Scotland until his father retired. Close to his mother, he was terrified of his father and had little real contact with him until adolescence. His mother thought him a sensitive child and considered taking him away from public school, where he was severely bullied, after his first year. But he stuck it out and began to study for the army, only to find his ambition thwarted by poor eyesight. He went to Cambridge to read law. A year later, the first World War broke out and he volunteered immediately, scraping into an army commission by memorizing the eye chart. Happy to be in the army at last, he none the less refused a regular commission at the end of the war because it meant a drop in rank, and returned to Cambridge. Almost immediately his father died. Though his mother was left comfortably off, he refused to 'sponge' on her because, unlike his father and brother, he hadn't won a scholarship to university and felt inferior to them. He left Cambridge, married his best friend's sister – my mother was his second marriage – and took a mediocre job in shipping. It was this that led him eventually to Hamburg . . .

'Well, there seem to have been attenuating circumstances to what you consider his failure.'

'Pride or lack of determination. He was a failure and that's all there is to it . . . '

'As a father to you, perhaps . . . '
'And as a husband.'
' . . . '
'A failure, yes . . . ' I feel myself sinking, contradictorily, in the silence as a memory returns unexpectedly and with force; the memory of sitting on his lap in the green armchair – his chair – in the smoking room while he read to me after lunch and let me eat the hard, coffee-soaked kernels of sugar at the bottom of his cup. It happened only when my mother was away, on one of those long summer holidays in Germany. I never knew why she went but I felt she had left me. Perhaps I felt I had driven her away and I needed him; and perhaps he needed me. At any rate, her absence allowed him to express an affection which, when she was there, remained firmly repressed. In the same way that my mother only seemed really loving when he wasn't present. 'There was no unity of love between them for me. In fact, I have no sense of them as a couple, as parents, as lovers . . . '
'Perhaps you didn't want to see them as a couple . . . '
'Not to see them together in bed?'
He makes no reply.
Again vague memories return. The large, seemingly dark bedroom – dark despite the three French windows overlooking the lawn which in fact made it one of the lightest rooms in the house – with the heavy double bed, mahogany wardrobe, chaise-longue, night table on the window side where my father slept and in the drawer, above the chamber-pot, the small black revolver. Why? To scare off intruders. Would he really use it? There were bullets loose in the drawer. The black, metallic object with its threat of wounding, killing, frightened me.
'He could use it to defend his bed?'
'More. I sense it as his instrument, with all the ambiguities of the word, with which he attacks my mother. His penis, I suppose . . . '
'To keep you away . . . '
'He's an oppressive figure and I'm too small for him.' Fleeting images arise – of him, silent and threatening behind his paper; of him stamping out angrily one morning to shoot a foal in the field, a foal hung on a wire fence with its guts trailing from a pierced belly. He swears. Another morning he comes down laughing instead, telling Ilse that I asked whether he played in bed with mummy the way I do with her before getting up . . .
Silence. It endures, perdures unbearably.
'It would be good if you said something . . . '
'If he said something . . . '

'Mmm . . . He never said anything, not to me anyway. He talked to others, he had a charm he could turn on with women . . . ' It reminds me of Ilse's account of his affair on our arrival in Amnersfield and of my mother's immediate return to Germany with me. 'I don't remember it, but as soon as she told me I felt something threatening, confusing was happening . . . '

' . . . '

'The moves back and forth . . . That time seems full of turmoil.'

'Wasn't it a time of great confusion in Germany? Didn't Hitler come to power shortly before you left for England?'

'Indeed!' I feel an extraordinary gratification at having my confusion linked to a socio-political conjuncture. 'In fact, my parents left Germany because of Hitler . . . '

'Uh-huh . . . '

I'm silent, aware that I'm not free-associating, only recalling memories. Then I say: 'No, I've got it wrong. They left because a tax agreement my grandmother, the baroness, had with the German authorities was about to expire.' I laugh. 'You might have guessed it. Money and chaos . . . '

The failure to remember this brings back a sense of confusion. I'm lost in a darkness of not knowing what they're doing, what they want. 'The family doesn't work,' I say suddenly. 'The only time I recall my parents acting together as a couple was when both were angry with me at once . . . '

I can see it still, the dark front hall with the black wood table held in place by a black pillar, empty of servants or parents as the door-bell rang. I ran quickly to open the door, exultant at being of use. A man stood there. "Is your mummy in?" "Yes," I said, "please come in and wait." I showed him into the hall and ran to find my mother. A couple of minutes later she returned white in the face. "That was a beggar, Alexander," she said to my father. And then, rounding on me: "How did you dare let a man like that in?" As they both started to scold I felt a terrible pang and ran across the fields to the spinney, convinced of my wrong-doing.

There's a silence, then he says: 'You may have identified with the beggar. You wanted something from the house you couldn't get.'

An interesting thought, I reflected. A rejection of privilege, an early identification with a different class. But I doubted it. The scene confirmed a deep sense of something else. 'Guilt . . . ' I say, but I don't know how to go on. 'There was something wrong with my childhood. I always felt split . . . '

The voice announced that we were passing over Geneva. 'On our left you can see Mt. Blanc. The weather in Rome is sunny, the temperature thirty degrees centigrade, eighty-five degrees fahrenheit. We shall be landing as scheduled at 18.50 hours local time . . . '

I looked down and thought I could just make out the thin white column of the *jet d'eau* where the city met the lake. Three and a half years of analysis and I was no nearer the end – just a little closer to the beginning, perhaps. The half dozen notebooks in front of me were filled with records – as accurate as I could make them – of memories, fears, desires, hatreds, which cried out for order, meaning – and which remained resolutely random and chaotic. A momentary illumination was soon overwhelmed by further confusion. Unfairly, I sometimes blamed P. himself. But I came to see that it was the analytic method itself which was the cause; the day-to-day experience of psychoanalysis was as far removed from the analyst's case history as the chaos of day-to-day living is from the novelist's finished work.

And yet something was happening, some flexing of emotion which I couldn't pin down to any particular aspect of the experience. Why – and if so, how – did this chaotic procedure work? I couldn't trace a pattern; it seemed as much unconscious as conscious, as though what was thrown up from the dark returned to the dark radically altered by its brief passage through daylight, though even of this I couldn't be sure. Yet I was filled with certainty that the people of my past had drawn closer, that I was seeing them more clearly. Perhaps some of the splits were healing over. Perhaps some of the anger which welled up destructively from hidden depths in that double-doored room found release from sustaining a distorted view of the past. Perhaps the confused and peculiar process was already repairing a vision which, while it loved with one eye and hated with the other, destroyed a large part of what it saw.

I turned again to the window and caught sight of the familiar snow-capped mountain which, thirty years ago as I lay on the lake-shore reading Gide, had summoned up dreams of a written world as eternal as the glimmering peak itself. I would be a writer, I told myself. 'What could be more exhilerating than to start from one's lived experience and, by the art of writing, recreate it for the reader as a general experience, without for all that losing its bitter taste of singularity?' I said to P. last Tuesday, omitting to add that I'd found the words in Sartre's book on Flaubert. 'As raw material for art my life would acquire a value it otherwise lacked. I would live to write, not write to live.'

He laughed. 'I'd say that you were trying through other means to reach the mother you loved. Weren't you just saying how happy you were with her in Geneva?'

'Oh yes, once,' I repeated, 'after Teddy Leroy's death. She wanted to go back. It was there they'd fled to from Amnersfield in their private plane, you see, it was there they'd been happy together until he started to die of cancer. And it was there, too, that I was happy with Simone...'

Through the window I saw Geneva fading into the darkening horizon, Mt. Blanc still white against the late afternoon sky; and I saw again Simone's cool eyes, flecked with brown like the leaves of dried flowers, as she looked across the distance at me and I, looking back, watched her moving slenderly, silently away.

'Have I told you about Simone? No... We were students together and I fell in love with her. Very deeply. After a year I had to return to England and she stayed in Geneva. I only saw her briefly again a couple of times and yet I went on loving her for the next eight years. I kept her alive in me, like an absent-presence, by writing...'

'An absent-presence, what do you mean?'

'I don't know. Being part of me without actually being there. Once when I was in her room alone I felt invaded by her presence in the things scattered about – a hairbrush, necklace, ordinary things that everyone more or less has. She was almost more real when she wasn't there...'

There's a long silence. I feel him about to say something, perhaps indeed he starts to speak, when I say: 'The absent-presence I've always known is my mother, isn't it?'

'Certainly that's what she was to you, wasn't she? I was wondering whether this wasn't an *imago* – an idealized image you internalized as a child.'

So obvious in itself, the discovery still comes as a shock. 'That's why I find my mother so difficult to write about. She's never totally there, I can't come to grips with her. You know, it's almost as though she were an absent-presence to herself...' I recall a chameleon-like quality about her that's perhaps characteristic of many older women in this society. In her relationship with men she took on their colours, their tastes, their interests and often I wondered who she really was to herself. 'Well, I never found out because two months after our return from Geneva she married a man who was about ten years older than me. And five years later she died.'

April 7, 1981

'And you never mourned her?' he asks.

'No. I don't think so.'

' . . . '

'No, I didn't. I'd got too used to losing her.'

I picked up another notebook from the tray. Below, the Alps were barren and inhospitable, unlike the glowing, snow-covered summit we had just left behind.

June 11, 1981

' . . . '

'Even then,' I say at last, 'as I lay looking across the lake, never sure which "I" was looking at the past, I suspected the dream was flawed . . . '

' . . . '

'As a writer, the first person comes hard. That can't surprise you. The problem doesn't arise as an anonymous interviewer . . . '

'Perhaps you prefer to remain the observer of your childhood feelings rather than to re-live them . . . '

'Perhaps, yes . . . It's no accident, I suppose, that, in writing, I choose to stand outside myself, as though I'm talking to an intimate other – which is how I feel to myself.'

Silence. Then he says, 'it brings to mind a child organizing and trying to comprehend isolated events and perceptions before it has an "I", while it is still a "you" . . . '

'Exactly. There's that distance, that split . . . Yes, *you* is the pronoun I most often use about myself. I never had a clearly defined "I" . . . '

'Or rather,' he says, 'you had two. One for your mother and one for Ilse.'

'And a third, then, in the space between the two. In adolescence, Isherwood was my model writer. A camera I, observing, not participating. Why? I ask myself now. Did I fear that when I tried to express myself it didn't work?'

'As a child you perhaps felt that your parents didn't value your expression of yourself,' he says.

'They didn't *hear* me, that's for sure!' As a five-year-old I started to write for that very reason, I recalled. During a game of hide-and-seek at one of those interminable tea parties that came round week after week, I got lost in a wood. The sensation of being alone, the idea of being able to wander by myself, leaving behind the organized games and the nannies on the lawn stirred something incommunicable in me. In the car on the way home I tried to tell my mother and Ilse. ''I'm glad you enjoyed the party, darling,'' my mother said, and Ilse, who wasn't listening, started to talk about what one of the nannies had said. Neither understood; my words fell outside myself like stones and were stuffed into other people's pockets and forgotten. For what I was trying to tell them was that in a clearing I had discovered a tree stump on which, glistening in the sun, an amber pendant of resin hung over a round, shiny stone. Looking at the pendant, rolling the stone between my fingers, I was suddenly happy. In some way they became a part of me and I of them . . .

'I can only think that it was to make real what they failed to understand which led me to write down the adventure. It gave me pleasure, a physical sense of achievement, as though every part of me were awakened and satisfied. And there was something tangible to show for my effort, unlike riding or tea parties . . . '

By the time I was seven or eight, I go on, I knew I was going to be a writer. I would write about an 'I' who wasn't the 'I' everyone else knew, would create a world that my parents would have to recognize as being more valid than theirs, a world of which, moreover, I was the author. I would elude the destiny they had in store for me by a self-assigned destiny far superior to anything they could conceive of. 'The only trouble, as you can imagine, was that I had nothing to write about.'

He's silent; his silences still worry me but I try to ignore them, waiting for an image or idea to emerge. I sense it first as an irritation on the dark back wall of the mind and then the memory of the moment when I tried to recreate the Aldershot tattoo with my lead soldiers springs forward to fill the void. I recall the episode, my father's sudden command to stand to attention as I turned on the gramophone under the table to play God Save the King. 'There was nothing unduly surprising about his brusqueness, I had pretty well come to expect it. What hurt was to find that I couldn't create something without him pulling it apart – and it wasn't even he, it was a duty beyond him, the National Anthem speaking through him. I had nightmares afterwards about having to go into the army, and my mother reassured me: when I was grown up, I would decide. I took little comfort in her words. Childhood was not much more than an anxious wait for manhood, a future I couldn't imagine but which frightened me. I'd never be a man, marrying, marching, making money . . . '

'You must have felt very humiliated,' he says with a warmth that comes as a surprise. 'Your father, you felt, didn't value what you had created.'

'No.'

There's a silence so long that at last he asks what I'm thinking.
'Nothing...'

'Why don't you just let yourself go?'

'I can't. There's something – a blackness I'm frightened of, it's like
that cesspit at the Manor which Bert had to pump out, where my father's
condoms used to block the pump. I feared falling into that stinking blackness. We're never going to get to the bottom of this. I need a structure in
which to operate...'

'A structure? What for?'

'To make sense of the disparate things thrown up here, to fit them into
the larger picture, instead of just going round and round...'

'Impose a structure to control black forces which you fear uncovering...'

'Black forces? The unconscious?...' Suddenly I recall another black
force, a line of village children, powerfully awkward in their best suits,
some of them twice my size, bearing down on me when the front gate
opened for their annual treat at the Manor. A few I knew by sight but not
to talk to; the rest were just faces, anxious and rough. Waiting alone at the
bend in the drive for the phalanx to begin its descent was a moment I very
much feared.

'And then, as they began to scatter through the garden on the treasure
hunt, I would feel a certain superiority, the superiority of belonging. They
were only here – in the garden, not the house, of course – because we were
giving them a treat. "This is *their* treasure hunt, darling, not yours," my
mother said. "You must help them..." As the afternoon wore on
amidst raucous shouts and moments of occasional bewilderment, superiority gave way again to loneliness and fear. Outside the walls, I knew, they
were stronger than me, doing things I couldn't do, working in the fields at
harvest time...'

'...'

'I suppose these social differences don't seem very important to you.
But to me they were very real... In fact, as I've said before, the servants
were the real human beings in my childhood whom I felt close to, sided
with. Of course, it was an ambiguous alliance because I knew I was the
little master...'

Still he says nothing.

'A role of inherent superiority which came to me from outside, from the
servants among others. Inside, however, I felt inherently inferior, inadequate to fill the role. That was the split...'

'In the servants' eyes you may not have been solely what you think,' he replies rapidly.

'Oh?'

'For them you may have been a child to be pitied – a poor little rich boy . . . '

For a moment I'm silenced; then I recognize that this is exactly what their interviews have shown. 'All the same, are you saying that my social role didn't come to me from outside?'

'Well, at that age I doubt whether you'd have felt the social role that exclusively.'

'What!' I expostulate. 'I've felt it intimately for as long as I can remember . . . ' Rather sharply, I recall some of the details he already knows, adding for good measure: 'When I was four or five, I was brusquely reprimanded by my father at lunch for speaking like Bert. To make it worse, my mother agreed. It made me understand pretty quickly that I wasn't to be like the gardener.'

'Yes, of course. All I wanted to say was that the idea of little master may have had other meanings for you.'

'Other than the basic split between social and individual reality, you mean?'

'Yes. You may have used the idea of superiority to console yourself for a sense of exclusion, for not having as much of your mother as you wanted.'

'I never had any of her,' I retort; and after a pause, add: 'What am I to make of interpretations that don't ring true?'

'They're only suggestions,' he responds mildly and thereupon falls into silence.

In his withdrawal I take comfort in the criticism that psychoanalysis refuses social reality – except to make you accept it. Abstract as it may seem to him, the inability to fill a social role, my hatred of English class rigidities and inherent superiorities, led me to some concrete choices; to flight from England over twenty years ago to Spain, an unknown country – yes, Franco's Spain! – where I hoped to become a writer and never again be recognized as belonging to a particular class. It was that or suffocate. And to my reconciliation with England many years later through the discovery of a new way of understanding and contesting English society – and of marxists actively engaged on the task . . .

'Your refusal of the social is a failure to recognize an important determinant,' I say. 'It's like your refusal of a structure, a theory, to understand how things are inter-related.'

He doesn't answer immediately; I wait in silence and eventually he says: 'I don't refuse the social, as you say. As a child you must certainly have felt yourself in an ambiguous situation. On the one hand, the servants no doubt considered you the little master. On the other – perhaps out of envy – they saw you also as a child to be pitied. And you probably felt that your parents saw you as neither . . . '

'Well, as long as we can agree on that. But you still refuse me the theoretical framework in which you're operating . . . '

'You sound as though you think I'm withholding information from you.'

'Of course. You hide more than you give away,' I reply without thought, taken aback by my sharpness of tone.

'Who am I?' he asks.

'You . . . I'm sorry.' I need to make amends. 'I know you're trying to help. Only the other day I was thinking, ''poor old you, sitting down here morning and night trying to help us all to get back out there to live a bit better. What a life you have!'''

'Perhaps it's what you felt about Ilse. Poor old you, having to devote your life to bringing up these children.'

'It's a good analogy.' My tenseness subsides. Is it because of sympathy for Ilse? Maybe. I float for a time, then remember that when I originally made the remark about him I added: ''and what's it all for?'' To get back out there to spend the day writing notes on these sessions, reading transcripts, wondering what to make of it all. Raw material – that's how I feel to myself.

'The other day I thought I'd put down on paper how I see myself. It went something like this: a fleeting face, shoulders bowed as though in constant retreat from the world. Works with the bureaucratic application of a bank clerk to keep anxiety on the other side of the bullet-proof glass. Relations kept to a minimum, as you'd expect, mainly the woman with whom he lives. Divorced, refuses to marry again, fearing commitment and repetition. Pessimistic – to the point of scraping the dish as though every meal were his last. Fanatic – to the point of bitterness at his inability to improve his tennis. Lazy – to the point of wishing for nothing better than – '

I hear P. laughing. 'It doesn't sound altogether like the you others see.'

'Ha! Perhaps not.' I hesitate for a moment, recognizing the detour I've made to avoid what I was going to say. 'But it remains a fact that you are withholding information from me. You know more about analytic theory than I.'

'But I don't know more about you than you know about yourself. Perhaps you want me to be a miracle-worker like your mother and provide solutions.'

'Mmm...I'm not asking for solutions. I'm trying to uncover the major determinants of this split vision.'

Silence.

'Like a historian, perhaps,' I add as an afterthought.

'Your own case history, I suppose. And what would you say if I turned you into one?'

Quite unexpectedly, irrationally, I reply: 'That you'd tied me down...'

'Like Ilse?'

'I suppose so...'

'And then you'd protest – and quite rightly.'

I reflect for a moment. 'Or, paradoxically, I might feel you had given me the assurance of a ready-made script.'

'Which is what you complain that your parents, your social role did for you in childhood...' He pauses. 'Well, it's not the way I work.'

'In any case, I'd set out immediately to re-write it. I want to be the historian of my own history, I suppose...'

Turning over the last peaks, the airliner settled into its long descent; on the horizon, shimmering hazily, I thought I could just make out the sea. I glanced at the last few pages.

March 30, 1983

A dream: I see the numbers 12 and 16 in front of me. A woman's voice says, 'You see, they're the same, except that the two is in-turned to the one and the six out-turned. You should be like the six...' I wake up laughing.

What are my associations, he asks predictably.

'It seems a joke. I'm being told to become out-going...'

'...'

'Ah! The two is lean, the six rounded, pregnant...'

'The two, your mother and Ilse turned towards you. The six, your mother turned away from you when pregnant...'

'Oh yes! They're turned towards the "I", but one reaches out to me while the other stretches away. They're with me, but not simultaneously.'

I start to add up the numbers to see if they come to something. No.

'Who is the woman who speaks?'

'I don't know... My mother? Telling me not to worry? Yes, not to worry about my father. She's standing with me against him.' Floating out of the darkness comes, once more, the vision of his stern, silent figure at the wheel as we set off to look at the prep-school which he has chosen. For days I had looked at his school pictures hung on the walls of my mother's dressing room – lines of boys in caps, scarves and sweaters with emblems emblazoned on them, staring arrogantly out of sepia backgrounds; was I supposed to become one of them?

'In the car they were both silent. My father had argued his case; my mother had reminded him of his own unhappiness at school. It only made him more adamant: spare the mother, spoil the child. My mother – and Ilse, too, apparently – opposed his view. It was then that I felt the split most sharply...'

'And you, most probably, wanted to stay at home, be the centre for your mother and displace your father,' P. puts in drily. '

'Ah-ha! Kill him and get into bed with her, that's the problem, is it?'

'Now you sound as though you're talking out of a textbook. All I'm suggesting again is that you wanted more of your mother than you could have...'

'Mothers,' I hear myself say, 'they're the cause of it all...'

There's a long silence, and then I recall that, as a child, I often felt – like my father, from whom I thought I got it – that women ''held men back''. The world of men was freedom, the world of women dependency. 'It's totally irrational, a male chauvinist attitude that I repudiate. And yet I recognize its roots deep in me.'

'Well, nannies often want to keep children dependent on them, don't they?'

'Yes, but it doesn't explain everything...' A vague image, no more than a shadow, of two women huddled together talking in whispers forms in my mind. 'This isn't for children's ears, I'm not supposed to know that they're saying bad things about my father.'

'What are they saying?'

'Talking about him and other women.'

'Who are they?'

'Ilse and – Mrs Carvell? My mother? They whisper in a corner. Plan in the shadows to get their revenge...'

'You make it sound fearful.'

'It is... It's another male chauvinist fear – the idea that women are subordinates whose only hope is to revolt and cut their dominators apart . . . ' I laugh defensively. 'On the one hand, my mother and Ilse stand with me against my father. On the other, they stand together without me against him – and I feel threatened as though I were he.'

'Uh-huh . . . '

'And with all this,' I continue, 'there's the idea that women are different, not human beings like men. Mysteries. I have a fascination to know how they feel to themselves.'

'The mysteries you wanted your mother to reveal.'

'Perhaps, perhaps . . . In any case, women carry the burden of men's mothers on their backs.'

'It's not exclusive—'

The rest is lost as I realize suddenly that the dream numbers add up to 10. 'One zero. The women have gone,' I hear myself say anxiously. 'I can't keep them going, it's too much . . . '

' . . . '

'I feel I have to keep them on course, like planets revolving round an emptiness. Hold them up there. And then I can't and they crash.'

'Crash?'

'Yes . . . ' I'm silent. 'The threat of crashes. They always seem to come . . . '

' . . . '

'The couple of times I went to Switzerland with my mother alone when I was five and six I imagined the train would crash, I saw a fair-haired girl in the dining car and, though I never said a word to her, I held her to me as I went to sleep, thinking, I'll die happy as long as she's here . . . Why – when I was looking forward to skiing, the happiest time of my childhood? I loved the freedom of the snow . . . '

'The girl who could replace your mother. You wouldn't die alone.'

'Ah!' The fear of being abandoned if things crashed: parents, Ilse, my mother . . .

Then he says: 'Perhaps you're fearing the "crash" of my leaving you for the Easter holiday.'

'Not at all,' I say irritably. Why does he always think I'm worried by his absence on holiday? 'I'll be pleased to have time to think about the book. As a matter of fact, I'm going to Amnersfield on Good Friday . . . '

'Uh-huh . . . '

'I haven't been back since I did the interviews ten years ago . . . ' Rapidly I recall the last time I saw the house, pushing through a gap in the hedge. 'It was a curious experience.'

'Why didn't you go to the door and say who you were?'
'I don't know. I couldn't . . .'
'What were you frightened of?'
'Frightened? I don't think I was frightened . . . Well, perhaps – of intruding.'
'But you intruded secretly.'
'Mmm . . . I suppose I wanted to see without being seen. I feel I belong there without belonging any more.'

After a pause, he says: 'Perhaps there are things about the past you don't want to see.'

'Still? Maybe . . . Anyway, this time I'm going openly.' I tell him about the demonstration from Greenham Common to the weapons factory at Amnersfield to protest against the nuclear arms race. 'I'll take my stand outside the Manor.'

He says nothing, and I lie there wondering whether he is sympathetic to CND. Probably not. He'll think my stand is some sort of infantile defiance. Against every prescription, I refuse to say what I'm thinking. After a time, he asks where my thoughts have gone.

'I was thinking about the book. I feel you're blocking me, bringing me back constantly to the irrational, infantile side of myself . . .'

In the ensuing silence, I realize that I have accused him of the irrationality which I have just committed. 'No, it's not you, it's in me. Actually, it's the emptiness of myself I feel.'

'You feel, perhaps, that you haven't anyone from the past inside you.'

'They're shadows. I can't hear them talking to me . . .' For a moment the phrase surprises me. Then a further meaning emerges: 'until they talk I can't recapture them, get them into the book.'

'Are there things you don't want to hear them say?'

'Ilse, my mother, telling me I must go? Is that it?' Suddenly, I'm looking down into a gaping hollow that, like the inside of a carcass, has opened up in me. 'Eviscerated,' I say.

'Could it be the loneliness of childhood, the sadness?'

'Ah!' As I hear the words I see a shadowy child dressed in white standing in the garden alone, watching, waiting, not knowing what to do. There is nothing, no one to play with. Even Bert is missing. I mustn't get dirty . . . But then another image superimposes itself. 'The garden is also my freedom. I can roam in it alone, be myself, the dirty little boy they don't want to know about . . .'

' . . .'

'I'm free without them. Perhaps it's *I* who doesn't want to talk to them and that's why they won't speak. Do you think that's it?'

'I don't know,' he says sympathetically. 'I haven't the answer. I'm not withholding something from you.'

'No, that wasn't what I was thinking.'

'Well, it's time . . . '

April 14

His car wasn't parked outside his house after the holiday. I looked up and down the Canonbury backwater lined with trees that are now suddenly in leaf. No, it wasn't there.

'And what did you think might have happened to it?'

'You'd taken it to the garage or perhaps you'd had a crash.'

'You feel I abandoned you and are angry, as you used to be with your mother.'

'Yes. I think I was often angry and wanted her to crash . . . And when she didn't, I brought the shutters down to exclude her.'

'You sound vengeful.'

'Um! You said once that the shutters protected me from pain. Now you're saying I'm vengeful.'

'They're not mutually exclusive. Perhaps you want to turn trauma into triumph – the victim who wants to become the victor . . . '

The words fall like dead weights. I say nothing. Thoughts flicker through my head. Is that what I'm trying to do? Triumph? Write a book to write them off? 'No, I don't believe it.'

Unexpectedly, his voice takes on a conversational tone. 'What purpose are you trying to achieve with the book?'

Relieved to find myself in a zone of normality, I outline the newly discovered aim of combining two different modes of enquiry – oral history and psychoanalysis – to uncover the past in as many of its layers as possible. 'At first, I thought I wanted your help to overcome the difficulty of writing about the past; now I see that the difficulty is part and parcel of the past. This "voyage of inner discovery", as I think you once called it, has to be combined with the account of the other voyage into the social past . . . '

'Uh-huh . . . ' After a time, he adds: 'Yes, through them you set out to discover the external objects; now, through analysis, you're seeking the internal objects.'

'And the two don't always coincide,' I reply. 'That's my split vision. Formed by the past, a person is also deformed by it.'

He doesn't reply at first. 'Well, it's not the past but what we make of the past that shapes our future and present,' he says firmly at last. 'But I can see that the two voyages share common elements of language and memory. Perhaps you could contrast them in the book.'

'Well . . . Yes, they're similar in reconstructing a remembered past, not the past as it actually was. In that respect, analysis is more limiting because it recreates the past only in the forms in which it was internalized or repressed. The infantile aspects . . . '

As I say it I see myself posing, a balloon in one hand, the other raised in a clenched fist salute, for my son's camera outside the Manor's front gate on Good Friday. Infantile, of course: but behind me, surprisingly, the gate is open . . .

'Yes. I wanted to tell you about this . . . '

It was one of those typical cold, wet days on the flatlands, and thousands of demonstrators had already arrived. We walked past the Manor. The gates were shut but, quite unexpectedly, I saw that the thick undergrowth and many of the trees which used to obscure the view had been cleared out and replaced by lawns; and it brought an instant sense of relief, as though a jungle had been cleared from my mind.

As more and more coaches went past it seemed that thirty years of isolation had come to an end. Nothing like this had surely happened in Amnersfield before, and I felt the walls behind which my childhood was spent beginning to crumble.

At noon we took up position in the chain of people still forming in protest along Nuclear Valley, as these flatlands have come to be called, when my son noticed that the Manor's front gate was open; on it a hand-written notice offered the use of lavatories to the demonstrators. Without hesitation, we walked down the front drive. There was the wide spread of lawn which Bert mowed with the donkey, and the hedge he planted on my mother's instructions, and then we were at the front door. An upper-class woman of my age, evidently the owner, opened it. I explained who we were. ''Come in, do come in,'' she said, extending a hand.

Hesitantly, we walked into the dark hallway of my youth and I was immediately overwhelmed by a sense of light and space. Nothing had changed and yet everything was different. The sombre, heavy staircase was now a lightly suspended white bannister ending in a colonial-style balustrade overlooking the hall which opened onto the large and once almost disused drawing room. Could this room, where my father had his desk, always have been so elegantly proportioned? So light and pleasing, with the French windows opening onto the expanse of lawn? I couldn't believe it. The owner showed us next door, and again I was overcome: the dark, low-ceilinged smoking room, where so much had happened in childhood, had been transformed into a bright and airy study. Was all this due simply to changing tastes, modern decor – or had I never seen what was really there? In my confusion, I knew I couldn't answer the question: but I felt a sense of delight, as though the sombre heaviness of childhood had been lifted from my shoulders and I was at peace with the house.

Then I noticed that the owner was wearing a badge which proclaimed: *Arms are for Linking*. She must have seen my surprise for she said: "Living here one can never forget. With the factory so close it's like living in the shadow of nuclear war . . . "

A momentary panic stirred in me: the tenuous peace could always blow up, someone had only to give an order, announce the inevitable and the world would crash beneath your feet. In the dark little smoking room across a chessboard . . . I caught myself in time, hearing her explain that her childhood had been spent in occupied Holland; the factory reminded her of the Nazis. "Liquidation, annihilation . . . ' "Yes . . . But in this case perhaps we can do something." I wanted to reach out to her. She smiled. "One must always hope.' I stretched out my hand. "Thank you very much. I'm pleased that you have the house . . . "

We left to rejoin the demonstration, and soon rockets announced that the human chain stretched unbroken to Greenham Common and CND balloons floated over the fences and hedges to cover the Manor's trees and lawns in a profusion of child-like colour. 'I felt then that every wall had tumbled down . . . '

He says nothing and, on the couch, I sense again both the amazement and peace of re-discovery.

'I came to protest at the past – the past that hangs like a nightmare over the present – and found that the Manor no longer represented the past.'

'Yes,' he says, 'where you expected destruction you found reconciliation. The authoritarian father of your childhood had become a person, a new owner, with whom you could identify.'

'The sort of reconciliation I could never have with him,' I say. 'We stood at opposite poles in everything.'

'You lost your father when you were young.'

'Lost? It was a relief when he left at the start of the war. It was the happiest time of my life. It was only when I lost my mother . . . Ah!' Suddenly the calm is shattered. 'There's the crash. Each time I was happy thinking I had her to myself, like during the war, she found another man and went off. Triumph into trauma, as you said.'

I wait for his affirmation which is a long time in coming. 'I said trauma into triumph,' he comments finally.

'Oh!' The observation silences me. 'What does it mean?'

'I don't know.'

In the silence the phrase forms and reforms across the screen of my mind. At last I say: 'Your words are right for my father's departure.'

'You reject the idea of losing your father, don't you? Perhaps you resented not having the loving father you wanted.'

'Maybe.'

'With the sort of father you wanted you might have become used to the idea of him being there with your mother while you followed in his footsteps.'

'Well, thank God, then! You know, he told me once that he'd have been a Nazi in Hitler's early days . . . But no, aren't you suggesting that if I'd had a model to emulate I might have filled the social role that always seemed alien?'

'Something like that.'

'Hmm! I don't much like it.'

'You didn't like your father, did you? You may have felt that your rage was responsible for his leaving.'

'No, no. My hostility was increased because he was responsible for making Ilse leave . . .'

In the silence, the pain begins to spread through me. Again I'm standing in the front drive, the same front drive as last Friday, though I can barely connect them, knowing that Ilse is about to leave. 'Rumours, snatches of conversation I only half understood, a row between mother and father behind closed doors, and then my mother told me that war was going to break out and Ilse must go. War – I didn't know what it meant. What would happen to us? . . .' I recall Ilse telling me about those last days. The Polish situation had become increasingly tense, everyone at the Manor was convinced that war was near. Alexander was already in uniform and waiting to leave, and Ilse had an overwhelming feeling that he was determined she should go. Janey was very worried that Ilse might be sent to a concentration camp. One evening she came into the nursery and said she had heard on the wireless that the German liner *Europa* was calling at Southampton the next day. ''I think you ought to go,'' she said, ''at least until things have sorted themselves out.'' Ilse had been packed for several days but this was the first notification that she had to leave. She was prepared to stay, had told Janey so; but the decision had been taken for her. The next morning, as I waited anxiously in the drive, William Carvell put her things in the car. Her last night at the Manor had been spent weighed down thinking of leaving us children and of the suffering she had known during the first World War. Janey kept me close to her as we said goodbye. Ilse was surprised how quietly I took it. Colin was very upset, he broke her heart more than I because I didn't express my feelings.

'I can still feel the pain, the loss and the fear. My father was to blame, I knew that in my heart. But there was nothing I could do. To complain, make a fuss would be wrong, would go against his orders. It was a serious situation and children had to keep quiet. My mother alone would have taken the risk of keeping Ilse, perhaps – but not he . . . '

And then he, too was gone. 'I don't remember any goodbyes. Nor did Bert: "He never said anything to us, never came out to the garden to say goodbye. Wouldn't have done, would he? I didn't know he'd left until someone in the house said, Well, the gaffer's gone . . . "

'So, in the space of a day or two my mother and I were alone . . . '

'Perhaps you felt guilt at that moment,' he says.

'Guilt? . . . Fear, yes. A few days later I was waiting in the same driveway and I ran forward to meet the car. "Mummy, war has just been declared, it was on the wireless. What's going to happen? . . . " She comforted me, but she looked anxious too. I didn't know then that Ilse had almost come back. The *Europa* never called at Southampton and she had gone by train to London. "Come back if you feel like it," Janey said when she rang from Victoria. She didn't know why she didn't . . . No, there wasn't any guilt.'

'I mean guilt because your father's and Ilse's departure meant that you could now have more of your mother . . . '

'Ah!' For a moment I can think of nothing but Ilse saying how that night, on the cross-Channel ferry, she had felt her heart breaking. She was leaving everything behind, would never return. "Never, never must I make any attempt to contact or show interest in you again, never in my whole life or yours . . . "

'I've gone beyond everything now into pain. It's a lasceration that's been with me since childhood, a loss, abandonment – I don't have the words, never have had. The pain just exists in me, and I can't give it any other expression. It's yet one more reason why I find it so difficult to write about my childhood . . .

'And you refuse to be consoled.'
'Yes, I've gone far beyond consolation . . .'

The plane turned slowly over the sea. 'In a few minutes,' the voice said, 'we shall be landing at Leonardo da Vinci, Rome. Please extinguish all smoking materials, fasten your seat belts and place your seats in an upright position. We hope you have enjoyed your flight and . . .'

Us

War has broken out, Janey said. Immediately I knew something frightening, terrible was happening – but what? I didn't understand. I felt Janey's sense of dread spreading through me – a dread related to Alexander's leaving and her own past in Germany. But I didn't know what to be frightened of, I simply felt this awful fear.

Colin paused. Within me I sensed the rising anguish but I didn't say anything. It seemed, he went on, as though his four-year-old's world had collapsed. Somehow he came to realize that Alexander was in danger, Janey's twin loyalties to Germany and England were in conflict and that nothing was certain any longer. Fear seemed everywhere, it hung cloyingly in the smell of rubber of his Mickey Mouse gas-mask and the heat against his face as his breath pushed the flaps out; he saw it in the terrifying appearance of others in their masks. It clung menacingly to the word rationing, he heard it wailing in the siren's alert, the upping and downing *whoooo oo ooo*, relived it each night with the blackout and the fear of showing a light. And then Jones's men came to dig the air raid shelter in the kitchen garden by the back door and he caught a glimmer of excitement beyond the fear: war meant aeroplanes and bombs but also chocolate biscuits stored among the provisions. Let's hope we have to spend time in there, I thought, because I'll be able to eat them! . . .

He laughed, the same childhood laugh. Behind him, through the window, the valley's slopes, cross-hatched with vines, lay peaceful in the morning sun. It's funny, he said, the war which started with such fear turned out to be one of the best times of my life.

—I know what you mean. But what made it so for you?

The main reason, I'm sure, was that Janey came out of her remote and distant world. Before the war there seemed a physical distance, lack of contact between us. In fact, I didn't feel close to anyone. Janey always seemed busy with other things, Alexander was a remote figure asleep behind his newspaper, you were not much less remote, and Ilse was a stern presence who didn't play with me. All I remember was feeling bored, isolated, out in the garden on my tricycle, the only time I looked forward to was Ilse's day off when Janey gave me a bath. She seemed close and relaxed then, the closest I got to anyone . . .

—And no memories of Ilse? That's surprising.

One, he replied, his first memory in life. Before being sent out to the garden for a routine period each morning he had to spend a long time on the pot, not allowed to move and feeling guilty if he wasn't able to perform. One morning he pedalled his tricycle under the nursery window and called to her that he wanted to go to the lavatory. Her reply was peremptory: Absolutely no! . . . It was his fault if he hadn't performed before going out. So he sat on his tricycle and messed himself, and the pleasure of the revenge remained with him, made him laugh even now.

I shared his pleasure, wishing I had had the same courage or defiance. But Colin, I remembered Ilse saying, was of a livelier and more independent nature than I. She would carry him in to wash his hands and as soon as she put him down he ran into the garden again, not to escape but to walk back in on his own. He refused to be carried, demanded attention as soon as he was awake in the morning, showed his feelings more openly than I. Perhaps she hadn't tied him down . . .

I don't remember being tied, no. But then I had her a much shorter time than you. I don't remember her leaving, any more than I remember Alexander's departure, and maybe they were part of my world collapsing. But very soon I had Janey almost to myself because Alexander's awesome presence had vanished, and you went to boarding school that first winter of the war, didn't you? Quite unexpectedly, Janey decided to go skiing in Switzerland as usual and took me with her. Looking back, it was a crazy thing to do, we might have got stranded somewhere for the rest of the war. The return across France in a blacked-out train was pretty tense, I remember.

Should I tell him, I wondered, what Ilse had said. Yes, of course.

He looked slightly surprised. Well, perhaps that had something to do with our going. I never heard or saw anything that suggested an affair but then Janey didn't spend much time with me. She took on that Swiss girl, Annie, who came back with us in place of Ilse. I didn't like her, but as Janey was so much closer to me by then it made less difference than it would have done before.

—Closer how?

Well, when we got back Janey started to do things she'd never done before, things in which for the first time I could take part. She worked in the garden, milked the cows, looked after the chickens. Because of petrol rationing, she bought a trap and we hitched the pony to it. Often she'd let me drive on the way to kindergarten and I got a kick out of that. When she went out to exercise the horses she took me along, and thanks to her I grew to love riding. Before, I'd always felt frightened because I couldn't control that pig of a pony. But she gave me confidence. I felt that she was there just for me. She was no longer tied up hunting or whatever else she did before the war, although hunting went on for a while during the winter of 1939-40. I remember being blooded – awful it was. Nobody told me what was happening, it was just part of a system in which you didn't ask or expect explanations. A mystery – something like the war, to be simultaneously feared and not feared . . .

In those early months, Colin went on, Janey displayed a new-found sense of initiative which was to remain with her throughout the war. Let's do this, that, she'd say, and off they'd go. She decided to break in *Midnight* as a draught animal, probably as a way of keeping at least one hunter to ride, and together they hitched him to a railway sleeper and made him drag it across the fields. Colin rode on the sleeper and Janey didn't care when he was shaken off and fell into cowpats. Together they made the Manor's first butter in the hand-turned wooden churn she bought; their excitement on at last seeing the yellow blobs forming in the cream remained with him still. She took to riding a bicycle; even her dress changed. In winter she wore a boiler suit and in summer overalls and a shirt. It was as though she were emerging as a person in her own right, he thought, no longer just Alexander's wife or the lady of the Manor, but as a working woman.

The intrusion of external authority still caused her considerable anxiety, however. When the War Agricultural Committee told her to get rid of the horses and plough the land; when the billeting officer ordered the Manor to take two evacuee families, the prospect seemed fearful. What did it all mean? She passed on her anxiety to Colin: our privacy, our fortress was about to be invaded. The very word evacuee became menacing. But it was the threat rather than the reality, for once the evacuees arrived, once the fields were ploughed, she accepted the fact as part of a new life which she was happy to be involved in.

Alexander's occasional home leaves also affected her and it was then, he recalled, that she instantly reverted to her old ways. No, now daddy's home we mustn't do this, can't do that . . . Things that hadn't troubled her suddenly again became matters of serious concern. Colin awaited Alexander's home-coming with a mixture of dread and pleasure that was summed up one afternoon when he set off happily across the fields to look for him in the spinney where, Janey said, he had gone shooting. Be careful he doesn't shoot you, she added, you'd better call out . . . As Colin walked across the field shouting, daddy! daddy! at the top of his voice, Alexander emerged from the undergrowth in a fury: his shooting had been spoiled, the pigeons scared away by his stupid shouting.

However frightening, these were infrequent interruptions in a life that now turned to new and fascinating rhythms. Every evening Janey tuned the radio's glowing green eye to German and British stations. She made no secret of her belief that an impartial view of the war could be had only by listening to both sides. She gave as much or little credit to one and the other, and there was again that sense in Colin of her divided loyalties . . .

—To such an extent that I was sometimes fascinated by the idea that she might be a spy, a traitor.

I remember that feeling, too. There were rumours about her, partly I suppose because of her past, partly because of the radio, partly because people were seeing the enemy everywhere. Aliens were being rounded up and imprisoned in camps, weren't they? One night an air-raid warden came in and played hell because the blackout curtains weren't properly drawn. Afterwards I recall comments from Bert and others that Janey wasn't British and didn't support the war effort. The curtains might have been left deliberately open to guide enemy bombers. It didn't worry me. At that time I would have justified anything she did, I was so happy to be part of her world. Before the war she really hadn't had a chance, you know. Now, the change in her made me feel free and uninhibited. No one expected anything of me any more, I could be myself. All my memories are of being with Janey and, when not with her, with Bert . .

It was a fiddle all right, course it was . . . When I came back from my medical, your mother said, It'll be all right . . . and your father, who was home on leave, told me he was going in to see them at the call-up place. That was getting on for a year after the war started. I'd seen it coming a long time. You watch it, it'll be our lot next, I used to tell the people who said there wasn't going to be no war. Hitler was one of the cleverest men in the world, I reckon, he'd got them all tied in knots. Especially old Chamberlain who came back in his topper waving that bit of paper – peace in our time and all that guff. Anyway, I got this letter – I've got it upstairs amongst the rubbish – saying that I'd be exempt from military service if I took up employment in agriculture . . .

For three months, until the Manor was officially classified as a farm, Bert had to work on a small-holding.

Your mother bought a couple of cows to make it a farm, you see, and then I came back. Your parents never asked if I wanted to stay or go, nothing. But a man's a bloody fool to go in the army if he can get out of it. It wasn't long after Dunkirk – a sad day that was, to think of a whole lot of us being driven out – and it looked as if we'd had our chips. Bloody Hitler'll be here in a fortnight, I used to say, and there were thousands who thought like me. He could have done it if he'd invaded then.

—Did you join the Home Guard or something?

What! They was only broomsticks round here, wasn't they? Broomsticks and bash 'em when they come into Amnersfield. No, there was nothing you could do but hope for the best. I made my will, but when I looked at the bank book I had nothing to bloody well leave . . .

I leafed through the transcripts I had brought for Colin; somewhere in my head Bert was singing:
> Underneath the spreading chestnut tree
> Neville Chamberlain said to me,
> If you want to get your gas-mask free
> Join the flipping ARP . . .

and laughing when I got the words right. But in the house there were half-spoken words and silences. Who should go, who be kept on? Only one of them might be exempted from the army if it could be shown that he was an agricultural worker. In her heart, it seemed that Janey favoured Carvell but calculation indicated that Bert's skills were more likely to convince the authorities . . .

It was all done very – discreetly, do you call it? Carvell recalled. Bert knew all about it and I wasn't supposed to know. But I soon put two and two together . . .

As the groom, Carvell thought he should have been given the cows to look after. But he loathed anything to do with gardening and wouldn't have taken it on even if asked. Most important of all, a family man of his age wasn't going to be called up, he thought.

Hunting continued during the first winter. But soon there wasn't food enough to keep more than two horses in the stables. He took one hunter away and the others were turned out in the fields. He never heard what happened to them because in the autumn of 1940 he went for his medical and was passed fit. It was too late then to do anything. He had to report to the army on his thirty-eighth birthday.

The evening before he left he went in to say goodbye to Janey. She was in the smoking room alone in her blue velvet evening dress, he could see her still. As he entered the room he felt as though a heavy stone had dropped. The atmosphere – it all seemed to have gone. You're leaving me, William, in the middle of the week, aren't you? . . . I don't know about leaving you, Madam, I answered. It's a case of having to because my job isn't deferred. I don't know how long I'll be gone, not long I hope, if we can get rid of this Hitler man . . . If it had been the captain I expect he'd have said, If it wasn't for these b. Germans or something. His last words to me in the harness room when he came to say goodbye were, Cheerio, William, if you have to go to war don't trust a German, not even a dead one . . . Why he said that, I don't know.

Carvell stood there in the smoking room looking at Janey and expecting a firm shake of the hand, a fiver pressed into it and a, Thank you for all you've done, let's hope we'll be together again soon . . . He'd been at the Manor seven and a half years but it could as well have been seventeen and a half years as far as he was concerned. A fiver would have been a lot of money to him. Many of the grooms who were in the army were having their wages paid while they were away.

Instead she said, You're leaving me on a Wednesday . . . Well, if that's the way you're looking at it, I am, Madam . . . And she handed me half my week's wages and nothing extra. It shook me rigid. I could have left the

Manor earlier to join the fire brigade and been exempt, but I was too loyal. Now I felt double-crossed. Nothing was done to keep me in my job and in the end I didn't even get a little present for all the time I'd been there. In fact, I thought less about the money than about her being sorry I was going. And if she had been sorry she'd have shown it by giving me something. That was what hurt . . .

Throughout the war she never wrote, not even a Christmas card. She seemed to have forgotten him completely. There had been too many wounds now for him ever to want to return to the Manor and, even had he wanted, his wife wouldn't have let him, he was sure. But in any case, there were no horses to go back to, were there?

—No . . .

Carvell's departure, I thought, was like a line drawn through the past; the uneasy transition from peace to wartime was finally concluded and nothing would be the same again. It had taken a year: the 'phoney war' of the freezing winter and chilly spring of 1940 had irremediably given way to a real, if still invisible war. On a clear September morning before I returned to boarding-school, Carvell took me out cubbing and the blue sky was peaceful. The huntsmen talked of the hundred or more enemy aircraft downed the previous day, but the Battle of Britain was being fought in other skies. Six weeks or so later, as I stood by the back door, home for good at last, the night sky forty miles away over London was burning red.

The Blitz brought back the evacuees, though in lesser numbers than at the start of the war when most had returned home after an unhappy few weeks' stay. With them came Nelly Wintermann and her daughter Lisel. Excepting Bert, all the pre-war staff had left and Janey had been hard put to find Mary and young Betty as maids. The Manor's centre of gravity, the kitchen, remained empty until small, plump Nelly came to fill it for the rest of the war . . .

I was so happy to come to the Manor House. It was the most richest house I have seen in England. My father had an antique shop in Vienna, so I understood correctly what was nice and what not. Before, I was in St. Albans. The bombing was so bad we had to sleep under the table. It was terrible. In the morning I had backache. It was autumn 1940 and I wrote to my sister who was working for Mrs. Huntley at Amnersfield. 'My lady got a good friend, she wants a cook, it's a lovely house . . . ' she wrote me. And so we moved.

Eighteen months before, in the last train carrying Jewish refugees from
Vienna, Nelly Winterman and her eleven-year-old daughter had reached
London. Her husband, a book-keeper, had left earlier on a single exit
permit for India where his brother had an import-export company. As
soon as it was possible she would join him there.

On arrival, she went to work cooking and cleaning house for a Jewish
family of furriers in the East End for £1 a week. Nelly had never worked for
anyone before. The woman of the house deducted 7/6d from her weekly
wage for Lisel's board, provided one bed without blankets for both of them,
and made Lisel clean the silver after school. Her meanness with food dis-
mayed Nelly. I was shocked that Jews treated us like that. I couldn't believe I
could hate anyone like I did her. The East End was shocking, too, dark and
dreary and covered in smoke . . . Nelly went to Bloomsbury House which
dealt with refugee affairs and, though desperate to remain with her daughter, accepted separation to escape the furriers. Finally, at an alderman's
house in St. Albans, she was reunited with her daughter and would have
happily stayed there had it not been for the Blitz which began in September.

At the Manor Madam was ever so sweet. She spoke German, her
behaviour was wonderful, she understood everything. She say to me one
day, It doesn't agree with me to call you Cornelia or Nelly. Can I call you
Cookie? . . . And that's the way it happened. Everyone call me that, in the
village as well. Every morning before breakfast about nine she talk with me
in the kitchen about what she want for lunch and what will come in from
the garden. Anything what I needed urgently I got, I had not to ask several
times . . .

Getting up at 6 a.m. to be ready an hour later when Bert brought in the
milk, which she poured into large aluminium containers in the larder, she
worked through until ten at night. Each Monday she made about 10 lbs. of
butter and every second day soft cream cheese. At 11 a.m. there was a tea-
break and the staff came in, Bert, Mrs Winteringham sometimes, Mary
and Betty. I got my cups out, I brought everything to the table but I left
them to talk. I wasn't very interested, my thoughts were far away . . .

Punctually at 1 p.m. Cookie had lunch on the table. Soup, meat, two
vegetables, fruit and cheese. Madam loved goulash, schnitzels, dump-
lings, salads, mayonnaise. I make very nice pastries, cheese soufflés. There
was everything except fish. The larder was full of fruit I had bottled. One
day she came in with some cherries. What a shame we haven't got sugar to
bottle these, she say to me. I take her to the cupboard and show her the
40lbs. of sugar we got there. She didn't know. It come from the parcels her

mother send from America. You wouldn't know there was a war. When I was in Vienna still, I was thinking so often that in England my child will go hungry. But never, never in the Manor House. We got everything . . .

After lunch, Cookie had a couple of hours off to clean her room and rest. Before four o'clock she was in the kitchen again baking because Madam liked scones with butter and jam for tea. Not long after, the milk came in again. So much cream! Cookie made apple fool, gooseberry fool, rhubarb fool. Then, while she was preparing dinner, she ran out to the stoke-hold several times to make sure the old-fashioned boiler was burning properly. She would hear Madam upstairs running her bath. Cookie, the water is lovely! she'd shout. And then she came down in a long dress, such lovely dresses she had. You could see she was a lady a mile away. Beautiful. In the daytime she wears a boiler suit, a check or white blouse, long pearls. Her hair – the same blond hair like yours, lighter maybe. Gold, I would say. Her hands always perfectly manicured, a lovely diamond ring. Like that she goes to milk the cows . . .

Before dinner she had a drink while she waited for Cookie to ring the bell to announce that the food was on the sideboard. Three courses, hors d'oeuvres or soup, meat – very often game – and a savoury. Between courses, Madam rang the bell and Cookie in a blue and white uniform and cap, or Betty in her parlour maid's uniform, cleared away. During the meal Madam drank wine, Liebfraumilch that she got in the town. There came boxes and boxes of wine, something I never touched . . .

—I remember the wine. But where did all this meat come from?

Madam got it, she got everything. A butcher comes in a van every day nearly. In Amnersfield there was not the strict things like in London.

—You mean she had some sort of fiddle . . .

I think so, I expect so. Madam was not short of money. Saturday we got paid and she had a purse in her hand – tiny little hands she had – and this purse she couldn't close, so much money she got for the wages. Madam paid me exactly £5 each week, I had not to pay for Lisel, not a penny. She was ever so good. I was two months there and Madam went to town and came home, and I got leather gloves with fur. Only two months I'd been in her service. She was like that, any happiness she could give me I got . . .

—And so, after dinner, what happened?

She would ring the bell and go back to the smoking room. When Betty was off, I brought in the coffee, a beautiful coffee service it was. Madam put down her book and we talked, she let me sit down. I could see she was relieved to talk with somebody. She was very lonely, never went out. I did everything for her, I looked after her because she was so lovely. Later, Madam was alone in the house with me – Betty had gone off to the army, Mary was ill – and I was on my feet all day and I loved it. I mean, she was the perfect person, I would do anything for her. Maybe I am childish. Betty, who was very lazy – not a nice thing to say – was a bit jealous. You're daft to do so much, she said, it's because you're foreigners. An English person wouldn't do it . . . And Lisel says, Mummy, you worked so hard there, don't you remember? . . . I say, No, I don't, I don't remember because I loved her . . .

ᘓ

April 19

Through the low farmhouse window I saw Colin walking between the rows of vines, stopping to examine the nubby grapes forming in clusters under the leaves. Beyond, under a blue sky, the soft slopes of the Sabine Hills shone in the early morning sun. Neither of us, in our different ways, I thought, had lost the need, learnt at Amnersfield, for contact with the earth; nor had either of us been able to remain in those wet and foggy flatlands. He had come to work in Italy not long after I went to Spain. Since then we had hardly seen each other; we had never been close. And yet – was there some destiny, or only coincidence, in our shared need for clarity of sky and heat-held landscapes?

I watched him coming in, his blond beard resplendent in the sun, to continue our talk which was interrupted when he was called to the village yesterday evening. As he came through the door he was saying, Some childhood memories you never šeem to get rid of, do you? I just picked up a respirator for vine spraying and that dread of my Mickey Mouse gasmask returned . . .

—I know what you mean. And yet, reading Cookie's account last night, I was struck again by how distant the war appeared. Such lashings of food for a start! No hardships – the contrary, rather! The war itself was little more than a backdrop against which we began to live a new life, it seemed . . .

Yes, once the initial fear was past, he replied. I remember when people started saying, They've been at London again . . . and the sirens went every night. Janey let me see the red glare in the dark over London and I was frightened that the war was coming our way. For a couple of nights we went down to the shelter. But Janey was fatalistic and we stopped going. After a while the shelter filled with water and we used to paddle in it for fun . . .

Although immediate danger receded and each succeeding day re-affirmed the security of his new world with Janey, each night, he recalled, brought trauma and chaos. A few hours after being put to bed he'd wake from some terrible nightmare screaming and vomiting. The doctor, whom Janey called in after a time, ordered light suppers, and a diet of smoked salmon became his habitual fare. It made no difference. The problem lay in an uneasy psyche, he was convinced – a reaction perhaps to Ilse's leaving and the collapse of his world at the start of the war.

Janey, who was always sympathetic when he was ill, mopped up and changed sheets without the slightest reproach or resentment. Annie, the Swiss girl, on the other hand used to give him hell. I must have been pretty disturbed because I developed a serious stutter which lasted some time and a forgetfulness that drove Janey mad. Soldiers, she'd fume, get shot at dawn for forgetting . . . But it made little difference.

—Cookie remembers that Annie was very bad to you. Wait a minute, I'll read what she says. Ah yes . . . Annie was a nice-looking girl, dark, quite pretty but she wasn't good to Colin. Nearly every night she leaves him. And he would be crying, very nervous he was. I used to go to his room, take him and wash him and bring him back to bed. Then Annie comes home and she behaves so hysterically, throws herself over his bed and cries, Colin, what happened to you again? Stop that crying . . . I say to Lisel, she is making him ill . . . He was terribly lonely, he came so often to me in the kitchen. All this rich house and everything, there was nothing Colin didn't have – and yet he was so poor in a way . . .

And Lisel, I went on, recalls that she and Cookie stayed up with you one night when Janey was away for a couple of days and Annie again wasn't about. Colin's screaming at night, she says – that's one memory I've never forgotten. It was like somebody – I wouldn't say tortured but closed in and who can't get out. Night after night, until we couldn't stand it any more. My mother felt so sorry for him that when Madam came back she told her what had happened. Your mother was aghast, called Annie in and there was a terrible row. It was the only time I ever heard your mother raise her voice or slam a door. After that Annie left. For a long time I don't think your mother knew what was happening . . .

I don't remember that, Colin said. Annie wasn't cut out to be a nanny and I don't think Janey liked her much. But there wasn't anything she could do because the war made it impossible for Annie to return to Switzerland. Why wasn't Annie around more at night, though?

—Don't you know?

He shook his head.

—She was fucking with Bert. I can remember him telling me about it. How she screamed when he broke her in in the spinney. I didn't know what he meant, he had to explain about the hymen. He didn't want to talk much about her when I went to interview him because his wife was there most of the time. But after a while he couldn't resist, he was still taken with her thirty years later. Beautiful she was, he said. Had the best pair of legs round here for a long way, like the river Thames – the higher you got the better the scenery . . . She used to have him off in the greenhouse while he stood there keeping an eye out, so he told me as a kid, until one day his wife stormed in and stood at the door until Annie left. Cookie knew all about the relationship. She didn't like Bert, felt he was hostile to her because she was Jewish. She used to see them meeting in the garden at night . . .

Well, that explains something, Colin laughed. I don't suppose you've been able to locate her, have you?

No, I replied. She, Marie the cook, and Johnson, the butler, were the only people I had found no leads to. No one knew for sure where they had gone from Amnersfield.

Colin went to make coffee and on his return I recalled that, with Annie's departure, his nightmares and vomiting had soon ended. Perhaps they were more connected with her than he had thought.

Yes, maybe I resented her replacing Ilse. Or resented another Ilse figure coming between Janey and me. Annie's departure seems in my memory to coincide with the war receding as a directly threatening force . . .

Instead, the enemy became a mysterious and invisible presence, he recalled, whose traces might unexpectedly be discovered lying in black strips of metal foil with a silver edge in the garden. We learnt, I don't know how, that it was dropped by German bombers but only much later that it was to confuse British radar. It had a strange fascination for us, like the piece of shrapnel you got from somewhere. That comes from the enemy, we'd say, as though it were imbued with some special power.

One typically grey English afternoon, however, the invisible became visible. A dark grey twin-engined shape broke out of low cloud a mile away and flew over the munitions factory across the fields, Colin remembered. The special *whumb-whumb* of German bomber engines gave the alert and you recognized it immediately. A Dornier reconnaissance bomber, it banked sharply to circle the factory a couple of times and then disappeared into the clouds as rapidly as it had come. I was very excited and frightened.

—Yes, it flew off and dropped its bombs on Reading. It was a market day and one bomb at least hit a Lyons corner house or shopping arcade, killing fifty or more people . . .

But Colin didn't remember that, any more than the two bombs that fell one night less than half a mile from the Manor: he slept through the whole thing. Only one exploded; the other made a clean-sided hole in the clay about three hundred yards from the house. After a few days, Bert said that he'd been to the edge and looked down and later we followed him, throwing stones into the hole to see how deep it was. The bomb was thought to be a dud; but when the disposal squad came and started to dig they found a time-bomb. The bugger's still ticking, the soldier who reached it said, if Bert was to be believed. When they blew it up with a roar that rattled all the windows, the explosion created a small but useful lake on which to sail our model boats.

Still, I said, those rare moments of threat had been nothing compared to the benefits of war. Petrol rationing, in all probability, had been the most important of these because it put an end to the round of children's social events which depended exclusively on the big houses. Life had other connections, other meanings now.

And other seasons, too! Colin interjected. A cycle that had a rhythm of its own and which began with the arrival of an old paraffin-run Fordson tractor to plough the fields. Sent by the War Agricultural Executive, the driver disobeyed strict instructions and let Colin ride on the tractor, though there was nothing but a strut to hang on to. The sight of the large spiked steel wheels advancing across the fallow and the curve of the fresh earth falling away from the plough behind entranced him. Then came seeding time and he'd stand with Bert on the plank at the back to make sure the golden waves of seed were running down the tines. That was nearly the end of him one day when the tractor lurched and he fell forward, doubled-up, under the seeder. Bert was upset and then relieved to see he was unhurt. You daft bugger, why didn't you hold on properly? Now hang on tight if you're going to stay up here . . .

The high point of the year and of my life, Colin recalled, was when the binder came in the autumn to cut the corn. Riding on the machine as it cut swaths round the field, I watched with fascination the standing crop in the centre begin to take on and accentuate the shape of the field's perimeter and waited for the beautiful scimitar in which it often ended. But the real excitement lay not in the shape but in the rabbits and hares holed up in the last of the corn. The tractor driver and Bert had their guns ready and they'd shoot a good number as they bolted . . .

During the threshing in winter half a dozen bags of grain would be spirited away. Bert would wait until no one was looking and dump a bag at a time somewhere out of sight to provide a little extra feed for the chickens. Later, he brought the bags into the house and hid them in the roof spaces which Janey had had opened by Jones's men so that incendiary bombs could be reached. Janey swore Colin to secrecy, an oath on which he felt his life depended, because it was a serious offence not to hand over all grain to the government . . .

—Bert could fix practically anything, couldn't he?

Oh, he was the one adult I could always go to to get things fixed or to ask advice. I must have spent half my waking hours with him in the early war years. He was my tutor and mentor, the only person I learnt anything from other than Janey.

Bert's main interest was nature. He taught me practically everything I knew about birds and bird's nesting: how to look for a nest, how to bring an egg down from a tree in my mouth and to blow it out. But his most insistently repeated lesson was that I must never take more than one egg from a nest. Encouraged by him, I kept canaries and racing pigeons. Bert was always ready to get out his bike, put the pigeons in a hamper and ride with me for three or four miles to let them loose. I was scared to death that the pigeons wouldn't fly home, but Bert would say, Don't worry, they'll be there by the time we get back . . . And they always were.

Strangely for someone who respected bird life, Bert also taught Colin to snare and kill birds in a trap of wood and bricks. More ingenious, if less immediately lethal, was his method of snaring pheasants by threading black cotton through grains of maize and attaching the thread to the trunk of a bush. As Bert probably expected, Colin's efforts in this direction proved fruitless, as did his attempts to catch rabbits in the snares Bert showed him how to set in the fields.

But in the autumn we caught rabbits enough, Colin went on. You must remember that better than me because they were your ferrets we used. I can see you still with a ferret inside your shirt . . .

—Yes, Bert showed me how to handle them. He master-minded the ferreting on Saturday afternoons, showed me how to set the nets, and which hole to put the ferret down. Janey came quite often with us. Bert's face was tense with excitement as we waited. Sitting on the warren above a hole, holding my breath and hearing my heart thump until, even louder, I heard the pounding of a rabbit bolting from below ground. Look out, there he goes! Bert shouted as a rabbit came leaping out. Quick as a flash he'd grab the rabbit entangled in the net and chop it behind the ears with the side of his hand. We used to eat a lot of rabbit pie during those years . . .

He used to do a lot for us, didn't he? Colin said. I remember once he took me to an Arsenal-Millwall football match in Reading. Bert was an Arsenal fan and encouraged his team by shouting, Up the field, Arse 'n all! . . . He delighted in childish refrains and ditties, do you remember? Better shot than Cowshot, Bagshot, Aldershot! he'd cry when I threw a stone that hit the target. Or sing: Little Robin Redbreast sat upon a pole, put his head between his legs and whistled God Save the King . . . Anyway, Arsenal won and we returned home delighted. But when I told Janey about the match I was surprised not to get her normal enthusiastic reaction. I felt an unspoken criticism, a certain resentment which recalled a similar feeling after I went with Bert to get my first racing pigeons. She seemed to disapprove, without wanting to say it openly, as though implying that I was stepping out of the established order. It was unusual because otherwise she never objected to my spending time with Bert on whom, after all, she had to rely enormously since he was the only man about.

—Bert always seemed to me a subversive. His comments about the Manor, about social situations, indicate, I think, both a fundamental hostility to and fear of authority. He wanted things to change but was fearful of committing himself to doing anything about it. Mockery, jokes, innuendo – that was about the limit of it. A subversive, not a revolutionary! In many respects I made his views my own . . .

He didn't talk to me much about things like that. But, looking back, I can see that involving me in football and racing pigeons, which were both working-class sports, was a form of subverting my sense of what was expected of me. Whether he did it for that purpose I don't know, but I recognized it in Janey's reaction without quite understanding why.

However, it was his joking, cautiously paternal side that appealed to Colin. There were the long daily conversations in the shed where, in winter, Colin watched him chopping kindling wood with a billhook and a tree trunk as a block. The thin sticks of kindling fell from the hook at tremendous speed. Those wartime winters were very cold and the pleasure of wood fires burning at night was one of Colin's sharpest memories. Following on the snowy winters came summers that were blissfully long and hot.

It was during these conversations that Bert sometimes made tantalizing remarks about sex. Once he said something very curious. Ah, but you have to pay for that, he replied to some question Colin had asked. It left him very puzzled. I couldn't see why you had to pay nor what. Did you have to hand over money? Or was it meant metaphorically? The latter, I now suspect. But every time I asked he would veer away. I can't think about that now, he'd say, and I found it all very tantalizing. By then, without doubt, Bert was the most important male influence on my life, much more important than Alexander who was just a hovering presence somewhere in the distance . . .

During the long afternoon break, while Colin worked in the vineyard (planted as a spare time pursuit three years ago and now bearing its first fruit), I transcribed the morning's tape. Then I turned again to the old transcripts I had piled on the table under the window. There was Bert, replying to a question about Janey during the war:

She changed so much, got so good I don't know how to describe it. Matey, pally, it was like talking to the missus or my brother. She was a lot happier than before, and so was I now your father wasn't there. We all mucked in together sort of thing. We had air raid warnings and all that to get used to, and we went down to the shelter, all of us together, you see, and there was no class distinction then. It was like one family . . .

Before long, at her suggestion, Bert was teaching her to milk. When she took hold of the teat I had to tell her, like any woman, you know, Well, just pull a bit like this . . . He laughed. She used to thoroughly enjoy herself when I was learning her and she became a good milker. And then she'd say, I'll milk this afternoon and you can have the time off . . . Can you imagine that before the war?

—What sort of things would she talk about?

Anything bar money – giving you money. Same as all of them. But otherwise she'd talk over various things, you children, what needed doing in the garden, the evacuee hostel she was in charge of, where she had to go. She was a lot happier because she was active, getting on her old bicycle and riding off to the hostel or messing about in the garden helping me pick apples and all that sort of thing. She was in with the roughs, you see, doing things.

It was, he thought, the clothes rationing which consolidated the change. She used to bring her clothes and shoes, some of them nearly new, to his wife to give to her friends in exchange for coupons. Once she brought a fur coat. She'd taken it to London to have it shortened and was offered £175 for it. She took twenty coupons from Mrs. Sell's sister-in-law instead and refused money as always. She just wanted to get clothes for you kids, she thought the world of you, she did. Before, she wouldn't have lowered herself to ask for something like coupons but the war changed things. And with that came the rest, her friendliness, her willingness to talk. She'd never go by in the morning without a chat, she became like one of us really . . .

—Was this something new in her or was it something more general?

It was a couple of years at least before we realized that things were changing everywhere. And then we could see that there wasn't going to be all this snobbery any more. Each time we got talking to the class they seemed different than they was years before – you could talk to them, they could talk to you. What turned it a lot was that there was tons of jobs about and no men available. The class had to eat humble pie to get the workers. It was the beginning of bringing them down to our level. And they never got back to where they'd been – and they never will . . .

—Not in the same way, at least. But even then you must have known that she was still the owner, had the money—

Of course there was a difference. I'd always call her Madam. Good morning, Madam, good afternoon, Madam, I'd say when she came up to milk, but only the first time and the last I saw her during the day. After that we just talked normally. Between the garden and the cows we spent a lot of time together. She always came with me when there was a cow to be mated because it was easier with two people. One of the cows always clamped her tail down tight. She asked me what to do. Get hold of her tail, I said, and pull it out the way . . . Well, she did and this little Jersey bull went over the top and hit her hand with his thing and she said, Oh! . . . and then he got it in and, would you believe it, he mated that cow seven times. And your mother kept saying, Come on, Billy, just one more for luck! . . . Poor bugger! I thought to myself . . . But she trusted me, your mother did, and if I said something was all right that was final as far as she was concerned.

While outside there was peace, within the house a running battle took its toll in the servants' quarters. Young Betty, who had started work at the Manor six months after the outbreak of war, took a hearty dislike to the newcomers, Cookie and Lisel, and sniped at them on every possible occasion.

It was Betty's first job on leaving school at fourteen and she found the hours from half-past six to nine at night very long. She hoovered and dusted, cleaned fireplaces, served at table, washed dishes, polished silver, got Colin's supper, turned down beds, put hot water bottles in and cold water jugs by them and – final task of the day – took in the drinks tray to the smoking room at nine. She had never realized how much work there was in a house like this – and all of it to keep only the three of you!

Her wage of 30s. a month didn't go far because prices began to leap: a pair of shoes which before the war cost 15s. soon rose to 27/6d. By the time she'd been to Reading after her pay day she was lucky if she had 2s. or 3s. left for the rest of the month. It wasn't the money as much as the loneliness that bothered her, though: none of the other servants at the Manor were her own age. She was the baby and would have remained so if Lisel, who was two years younger, hadn't arrived.

But Lisel, who now became known as Elizabeth or Lizzie, wasn't a servant. She was a little madam and I didn't like her. She was attractive all right, with dark, dark eyes and lots of puppy fat, but spoilt and selfish. Like an only child often is. I was a bit jealous of her because she was made more of than me in a way . . .

And this was true, for Janey favoured the newcomer: the sewing machine which had been in the servants' sitting room was moved, on her instructions, to Lizzie's bedroom, and Janey gave her a radio. Betty had nothing like this. Unable to take out her jealousy on Lizzie she directed it at Cookie instead.

I know I used to be very unkind to her. She was a funny old thing. She didn't speak much English and I couldn't understand her. She seemed to work an awful lot, but really she fiddled about and didn't get on with it. She always wore a queer cap with strings to it, and some of her cooking I didn't take to. Peas and beans dripping in butter, wine in red cabbage which should have been pickled, and once she even cooked pea pods before they filled out...

Betty maintained that she couldn't tell whether Cookie was German or Austrian. I was patriotic and resented her as a foreigner. Once the radio was playing Tales from the Vienna Woods, and Cookie said, Oh, that's lovely, it reminds me of home...And I said, Blooming German rubbish! It was the sort of thing you can imagine a kid saying, the sort of thing I wouldn't dream of saying today...

Poor old Cookie, she used to go round deep in thought, thinking of her husband or the relatives she'd had to leave behind. Maria, she used to call me, Maria, I'm so sad...She told me that some of her relatives had been killed, told me about the Jews and how awful it was. Her face would be drawn, you could see how she had suffered. She lived for the war to end. But she was happy to be in England with Elizabeth and know that they were safe. It wasn't often she spoke about her sadness, most of the time she'd laugh and joke with us. I followed the war news a bit on the radio and in the paper and I'd explain to her what was happening. I could always get her to understand. Otherwise none of us discussed the war much. Some nights we might say, Wonder if we'll get any over tonight...Or pass the occasional comment about the bombing the day before. But it didn't make anyone down in the dumps, if you know what I mean. I suppose we all thought we were going to win in one thing or another and that was it...

Mary, who had been in service for many years, returned to Amnersfield at the start of the war and began work at the Manor shortly afterwards. But within a few months she fell ill with suspected TB. She was off sick for six months and Janey made up her wages. She wasn't obliged to, no one in any of the other houses where she had worked would have done it, Mary was sure. But mummy was much more friendly than any of them, a jolly nice person to work for. Very kind and straightforward. I liked her from the start and she must have liked me to do what she did...

Betty didn't like foreigners, I could see it. She was jealous of Lisel. She made speeches at the table as I am carving the food and one day we had a terrible argument. These foreign people, she say, terrible remarks, and slamming the doors and taking away things. And I couldn't bear this language and I went to the drawing room and told Madam that I am leaving. Told her the situation. Next day, in the morning, your mother was ringing the bell, and the whole staff was to come in. Bert, Betty, Annie, Maria. We all stand around, it was like a court case. Your mother told Betty and everyone that if they want to go out of her service they can, but that I stay. From that time on there was peace. Betty never said anything more. Now she comes to visit me, invites me to her house . . .

Not many weeks after her arrival, Lizzie remembered, Janey announced the news, which she continued to repeat with some insistence thereafter, that her oldest son was coming home from boarding school to live. For a month Lizzie had it drummed into her: master Ronnie is coming, you've got to be quiet, you mustn't disturb him or get in his way. Don't touch anything of his when he's here . . . She was awe-struck and didn't know what to expect.

This was not the first of her shocks and surprises since arriving at the Manor. The place seemed so enormous at first, in comparison to what she had been used to, that she thought of it as a palace full of servants and riches. There were prohibitions attached: she wasn't allowed to wander round the house or go into the front garden; she wasn't to speak to the lady of the house unless spoken to, or to little master Colin; she mustn't under any circumstances go into the nursery. She could understand that she wasn't allowed on the lawn because in Vienna there were signs everywhere saying, Keep off the Grass; but she found it difficult to understand why she wasn't allowed into the nursery, and it took her a long time to get used to it. Yet, instinctively, she knew she had to accept it because, after being thrown out of her country, it was wonderful to have a roof over their heads among friendly people. I realized that we were dependent on my mother being able to work and on your mother's kindness in having us there. We were in a different country with different rules. Until we came to the Manor House we had never known what servants and class were. I thought of this master Ronnie who was coming as master of the house. Your mother was alone and she was going to be joined by a young man. And then a boy who was two years younger than me arrived, a very snooty boy who didn't say Good morning, who wouldn't even answer sometimes when I spoke. You just pushed past. I don't know who you thought I was. I was more frightened of you than of your mother because she at least spoke nicely to me. You probably thought I was just your mother's cook's daughter. You were very stern, we never saw you smile or anything, you just went striding out of the back door by the kitchen without a word. From the window of my room where I sat at the sewing machine I'd catch a glimpse of you in the yard, or I'd see you go into the dining room with your mother, a blond boy in grey shorts and jacket. But there was one thing that impressed me. I remember how your mother spoiled Colin, but the moment you arrived he was almost forgotten. You were the apple of her eye. I don't know whether this was because you'd just come home from boarding school . . .

'I felt I had no place at home, I'd done the wrong thing. My mother had rescued me, and that's what I had been praying for, but now I felt guilty. A boy of my class should have been tough enough to stick it out. I'd failed the role once again.'

'You felt guilty perhaps about being able to have more of your mother while your father was away,' P. replied.

'Displaced him at last? I was certainly terrified of what he would think of my weakness, failure . . . ' Throughout the first two terms of misery, I knew that he would never agree to my being taken away from Pinewood unless . . . unless the war turned threatening. As it was, the war seemed barely to be happening. 'A boy, as lonely and desperate as I, climbed into my dormitory bed each morning and we held each other tight, finding a human warmth which, for the rest of the twenty-four hours, seemed denied to us. Another boy, an East End evacuee, ran away. His sadness, loneliness, made him a friend and I spent hours watching him draw. But then he fled. Not surprisingly, as I can see now, I never thought of following his example.'

All this was met by silence.

'That school was only ten miles from Amnersfield, you know. It was the same one that my parents visited before the war, but it had been evacuated to a country house. I could have got home easily enough, even if it meant walking. Instead, I wrote anguished, homesick letters to my mother . . . '

Standing on the frost-hardened school lawn, I watched the older boys kicking a rugger ball around. I was hollow, bloody inside, as though someone had mangled the last protective inner lining. I had just turned nine, and I knew there was nothing I could do. That was the age she must have agreed with Alexander to send me away; the cold froze my guts but didn't numb the wound which kept throbbing with a thin flow of hope.

Left to herself she wouldn't have sent me, I thought; my going was still Alexander's affair. As she took me to start my first term, we drove past Amnersfield village school and I looked with longing at the kids in the playground. 'I wish I could be like them,' I said. I knew the wish was unrealizable; but I knew also that if Janey wanted to she could rescue me. For the first two terms, however, all my letters were met with pleas to stick it out because she was unsure what to do.

'During the summer term the God-sent miracle I'd been waiting for suddenly happened: Dunkirk. Even my father couldn't deny the gravity of the situation. Each morning and evening I prayed that the Germans would win the war and I could go home. The Germans didn't have boarding schools for boys of my age, my mother said. Moreover, if the Germans won the war it wouldn't be the tragedy the English imagined. She knew the Germans and was quite ready to live among them again. So there was no danger on that score...'

But instead of defeat, Dunkirk turned out a victory, or so the masters and Jenkins major, captain of cricket, agreed. There were thanksgiving prayers to prove it, moreover. Janey made no move in the face of this startling turn-about.

'By the start of the Christmas term my faith in the war's miracles had lessened. Then came the Blitz and hope was revived. In mid-November, as the Germans made for Coventry and then Birmingham, the night was filled with the unmistakable *whumb-whumb* of the bombers and I lay awake praying that a bomb would drop on the school and finish it all. The crash that would solve everything, you see. I didn't see myself dead – just fleeing the ruins, justified by the rubble...'

I waited for P. to say something, remembering that the bomb never fell, the planes went away, the letters of misery began again with even more desperation. It had been such a close thing, was the opportunity to be allowed to escape? Not a sentence must let Janey believe that I was willing to fight on alone. 'I was going to prove to her that the world was too big, too hostile, that only she could rescue me...'

'...'

'Well, I'll finish the story. When the headmaster called me in after prep and said, in a human sort of voice, "Ah, Fraser, your mother intends to remove you from the school because of the bombing... Ah, I told her not a single enemy plane has flown over the school for the last three weeks..." I just said, "Yes, sir, yes, sir," as though, despite my heart's pounding, all this had nothing to do with me. It didn't matter what the

Caput said now, Janey was superior to him. "Yes, sir, my mother . . . " and left it at that, my voice resigned to what had been decided from above.

'Once we were home, my mother made me promise that I would never regret the decision, a promise I solemnly gave. I think she was frightened by the enormity of what she had done and her sole justification lay in restoring my happiness. As it was, times were too grave for my father to make a fuss, the thing had been done and could hardly be reversed . . . '

After a moment, P. said: 'She colluded with you against your father . . . '

'Well . . . If you want to put it like that, yes. During the war I felt I . . . ' I searched for words, conscious of the ones which came to mind and which I didn't want to use . . . 'felt I was her equal. Or rather the man of the house.'

'You could be the master – or rather perhaps phantasize being the master – because your father was away.'

'The master of my mother. Yes . . . '

After a while, when you got used to being at home, you changed. Before that you were definitely on the other side of the fence. A bit, Come here, do what you're told, sort of thing, Betty recalled. As though you were the man of the house . . .

But once you began to go to that day school in Reading you became quite jolly and light-hearted. A bit of a scruff, really. I was surprised, I expected to see you dressed up tidy because you had the money, but you often looked worse than a village boy when you were at home. You wore trousers with holes in them, a big roll-neck jersey your mother knitted and which didn't fit nicely, and men's heavy Wellingtons with the tops turned down in which you trudged along. A mop of hair, not so much long as stood up – Tommy Steele fashion, you know. Your mother didn't seem to worry much.

You were a bit lonely, though, until Ron Jones, the carpenter's son, started to come down. Colin was too young to be a friend, so I think you were glad of me to come through to the playroom and chat in the evening when your mother was having a bath. We used to talk about books. I'd enjoyed reading from my school days. You lent me my first Zane Grey and after that I read all the others you had. There weren't any other amusements except the wireless in the servants' sitting room, knitting or sewing. Once you got very excited about Rider Haggard's *She* and I couldn't wait to read it after you. You used to charge me a halfpenny to borrow three books . . .

—Did I? Why didn't you tell me to go to hell?

Well, I knew it was wrong of me to be talking to you at all.

—Why?

Because you were who you were. I felt dreadful about it. You were master Ronnie and I was made to feel I shouldn't be there wasting your time. I should have been getting on with my own work. It wasn't you that made me feel like that, you were friendly then, like a mate. But when you were with your mother you wouldn't ever really speak to me, it was maid and master then . . .

—There were two different boys . . .

I wouldn't say that, but you had to behave differently. You weren't frightened of your mother but you knew it was wrong to be so friendly with me when she was around. You were on your best behaviour then, you showed her a far more serious side than you did to other people. When we were in the playroom together you were human, free and easy, I'd say, you could talk as you liked. But you'd talk more as a gentleman when you were with your mother . . .

—So there was still a clear dividing line between family and servants?

Those heavy swing doors divided the two sides, didn't they? I was the maid and that's all there was to it. I don't think I actually felt inferior but I was in a way. I was paid to be there, after all . . .

Being let run was the finest thing that could have happened to you, Bert recalled. You was opening up, more like the local children. You played with them as though you was one of them instead of the Lord of the Manor's son. Your mother always wanted you children to be happy, and when the war came and your father and Ilse were gone, she let you have your head. She was pleased to think you was enjoying yourself, she always had a smile when you got up to a bit of devilment. She'd say to me, Oh, Ronnie's doing so and so, Bert, he's happy with the other children . . . Before you were never allowed to mix and now you were one of the roughs. There was a vast change from the little Sir Echo you'd been before . . .

The sun was setting behind the cypresses on the distant crest; beneath them, the rows of vines were already in shadow. The hills lay smooth and serene as breasts against the purple sky. We sat in silence on the terrace, absorbing the landscape, absorbed into it. At last Colin said how often he longed to return to that complete childhood simplicity, that sense of freedom in the fields, hedgerows and woods of the war. Those long hot summers, longer and hotter than any we had known in England, when large parties of us cycled down to the weir and swam in the water where the weeds slid over our legs like a drowned man's hair. Or those Saturday afternoons, do you remember? In the large field where Janey and I watched Ron Jones and you flying the gliders you'd built, and time seemed suspended...

—Yes... The brightly varnished gliders built on the workbench in my bedroom during the winter under Ron's watchful but unobtrusive eye, soared upwards in memory again until they were no more than dots in the sky and we chased across the fields after them...

The Manor seemed suddenly to have opened its gates to the world, Colin went on. Every evening villagers came to fetch the butter and milk Janey gave away. She wasn't allowed to sell dairy produce unless she became a registered producer committed to supply customers on a regular basis, and so she distributed it free. In return there were always those few extra gallons of petrol, pounds of sugar, bags of cattle feed or whatever. This grey or black market created a new network of dependencies which brought the Manor and village closer together, and when Colin started to roam the village and play with the kids Janey made no attempt to stop him. His best friend became Wally Tines, the garage owner's son.

The garage was nothing more than a green shed and a single green petrol pump with two glass jars on either side which filled and emptied as the hand pump was operated. Colin used to help Wally pump petrol, and one day Lady Melbray drew up. She was shocked to find Colin serving her and told Janey, who laughed and thought it was a good joke. For Lady Melbray times hadn't changed.

Inside the open-rafted shed there was total confusion. The workbench was littered with tools and bits and pieces of every description. From somewhere Wally got hold of blank army cartridges and amidst the clutter he and I would take the powder out and put the cartridge in a vice. One or other of us hit the percussion cap with a hammer and there'd be a tremendous explosion, until one day a cartridge exploded before all the powder had been removed. When the smoke cleared I saw that Wally's face was singed. How we didn't kill or blind ourselves I really don't know . . .

In fact, there were very few times when anyone tried to stop him doing himself or others serious injury. There wasn't a roof at the Manor Colin didn't climb with Wally. It was dangerous and they broke a lot of tiles. But Janey only said, Oh, drat it! I wish you wouldn't go up there all the time . . . And when we learnt that calcium carbide, freely available at the village shop, made an excellent explosive, Janey never attempted to stop us. The blast of tightly-sealed bottles exploding in the garden can hardly have escaped her, can it? Later on, when I developed a passion for axes, she brought me one and I cut down a number of trees in the garden. I was surprised how easily I could get through quite thick trunks. She didn't mind. It wasn't until I cut my leg one day that she stopped me.

—And what about shooting?

That was the most dangerous of all. We used to shoot our airguns across paths and round the house without thinking twice. One of our games, if you remember, was to ricochet pellets off the walls and someone could have been badly hurt . . . As it was, there was a nasty incident one day when Dolcie, Joyce, Bert's oldest girl, and Colin were in the garden and Dolcie said, Let's play hunters! You be the hunter, Colin, and we'll be the rabbits . . . So he cocked his gun and as a matter of habit put a double *cupton* – which was Berkshire for double cupped one, a type of pellet – into the barrel. As they jumped round on the grass he took aim and fired. Ow! Joyce cried, you've shot me! . . . I can't have, he said, but there was this dark blue hole in her leg just above the knee with a little trickle of blood coming out. Colin was terrified. Joyce was taken straight to hospital and operated on, and they found the double *cupton* had flattened itself against the bone.

Janey confiscated my gun for a month, which I felt was perfectly just, but without recriminations. Bert was very good about it, too. I remember telling you, Ronnie, that I'd shot Joyce and you answered, Oh yes . . . You didn't seem to care one way or the other. You were in one of your withdrawn, unenthusiastic periods, as Janey called them . . .

—Mmm . . . Perhaps we'll leave that for later . . . My laugh rang a little hollow, echoing a numbness, a sense of isolation I wasn't ready to confront with him yet. Instead, I asked, Did your village friends used to come into the house? . . . He thought for a moment:

No, I don't remember that they did. We played outside. I don't think anything was said about it, perhaps it was just understood. On a couple of occasions Janey told me off for talking like them and I understood that it was common, that as a child of the Manor House 'one didn't do that sort of thing . . . '

—I was luckier than you, perhaps. Ron Jones used to come down to the house almost every night . . . First to fetch milk for his father, Harvey Jones, the village builder, I recalled, and then for a fortnight while he was painting the dining room. When there were workmen about I was never far away. One day he showed me a solid model Spitfire he had made from a bit of discarded deal in his father's workshop. I couldn't understand how a three-dimensional model could be built from two-dimensional plans. He said he would show me and one Saturday afternoon I went up to his house.

Was that how it had started, Colin asked.

—Yes. Ron knew so many things, there wasn't 'a tool in his father's workshop he couldn't use. He was sixteen, five years older than me, and he fired me with the idea of doing what he could do, the first time I'd found anyone I wanted to emulate. It wasn't long before I had a workbench set up in my bedroom and Ron was coming down every evening to make model planes. His were so good that he sold them; mine were those of an eleven-year-old who had never used his hands before. But he never told me what to do, never gave advice unless asked. If I wanted to know something he showed me with patience and without pretence. He was a challenge to me to prove what I could do rather than be. Just from the way he looked at my model I knew what he was thinking. Came out all right this time, he'd say. But he never made any compliments to me as a person, never gave much sign of thinking about me at all. I've always felt that he taught me not only to use my hands but, by example, the certainty of one's self that comes with knowing how to make and shape and build. He freed me to become myself . . .

I hadn't realized until now, hearing the way you describe your friendship with him, that the war was as important to you as it was to me. Something totally new . . .

—Totally liberating. I've been surprised to discover how much we share. We weren't shaped for the conformities of county life, were we?

It doesn't seem like it, no.

—I've often thought, childishly no doubt, that life in Britain could have been revolutionized as a result of that wartime experience. Instead, the ice-age came. The futile Imperial posturing, the great power pretence, the drainage and wastage of the cold war. By the '50s there seemed no hope and I left.

And later I followed you, he said. But not everything during the war was happy for you. You had an awful education at Hormel's day school, didn't you?

—Yes, I know. It was a hopeless school but I didn't say anything and Janey didn't seem to care. Do you remember old Hormel? The one large room where the older boys sat? There was no schedule, was there? It all depended on what Hormel had in mind for the day. He was the only teacher and drink was getting the worst of him, I think. We spent hours drawing coloured maps, learning the pence table and writing English compositions while he was off somewhere. Thanks to him I've never forgotten that 100d. made 8/4d. But he didn't teach arithmetic, let alone geometry or algebra. French was hardly embarked on and history oddly neglected. As for Latin, that was a dead language. Learn to speak and write English, a living language, he roared. There came a pause and loyal hearts knew what to expect: If that is good enough for Mr Churchill, it's good enough for me . . .

Sometimes, to heighten our appreciation of the English language, he would come into class and, to a general sign of relief that the pence table could be put aside, announce that he was going to read. He used only one source for our edification: the *Reader's Digest*. In tones that suggested Macaulay, he declaimed yet another People I have Known story, which he was especially partial to, as we listened with rapt attention in the hope of encouraging him to while away the whole afternoon. I was less keen on his instructions in hygiene which was another of his time-taking subjects. Cleanliness is next to Godliness, he'd bellow, as he embarked on a lesson in blowing our noses. Using a handkerchief forces the mucus back into the head. Do it the way I learnt as a boy. Thumb and forefinger holding the nose and blow – onto the ground. That's the healthy way . . . And once, to illustrate his point that manure was exceedingly clean, he related that he had eaten three pounds of horse dung as a boy in Ireland . . .

Colin laughed. His wife must have taken heart from that with those nauseating stews of meat fat and cabbage which, for reasons known only to herself, she cooked in the newspaper the butcher had wrapped it in. Lunch was the only ordeal he recalled. Not to stomach her cooking was an insult to Hormel's Preparatory School for Boys; to leave anything on the plate or pass it to another boy was strictly forbidden. Getting rid of the disgusting stuff under Hormel's wary eye and luxuriant, angry eyebrows was a frightening experience. Happily for the day-boys there were half a dozen boarders so starved that they would eat anything. Despite every prohibition, bits of stew fled from plate to plate in their paper wrapping . . .

—Yes, I remember it only too well. What a school – it ran on a miracle a day! Perhaps there wouldn't be stew or old Hormel might forget to call us in from play or talk the whole afternoon away. Alexander came home on a brief leave once and I was terrified. What shall I tell him? I asked Janey. Tell him you're happy, that's all you have to say . . . It seemed an inadequate answer to gloss over my failure to last out at Pinewood or to explain the vagaries of Hormel's. But it was also true. I was happy, happy to cycle ten miles a day to school and back, happy to think that when I got home Ron would soon be waiting to start work upstairs. School and home were extensions of each other, and for the first time I began to develop without being aware of the process, without concern for the future.

But, of course, the future caught up with me. No amount of happiness could get me through the Common Entrance exam to public school. When Janey confronted Hormel he had his reply ready: Mr Churchill couldn't answer a single question on his Latin entrance paper, Mrs Fraser, you know. But he learnt English. What greater master of the living word is there today? What greater man in short? . . . Unlike Churchill, for obvious reasons, my ignorance proved no virtue and I failed the exam. Then I really had to work and my best teacher was the local village schoolmaster. He got me through . . .

It was quite dark now, a warm moonless night. Moths fluttered round the yellow lamp, beating their wings hopelessly against the glass. The sound recalled some immolatory flight from those years that I couldn't place. I got up to change the tape, hearing Colin say how consistently inconsistent Janey had been in many ways. She had repeated my experiences with him. First to Pinewood when he was eight, then to Hormel's. He could remember the horror of Pinewood as though it were yesterday . . .

Night after night he woke up with nightmares of whirling through space, terrified of being lost in nothingness. His screams woke the other boys in the dormitory. During the day he suffered from a constant physical tightness, a pain in the chest which he could feel to this day when something was wrong. He felt totally distracted from his surroundings, totally absorbed by home which took on a mystical aura. Janey wrote to him almost every day and her letters became a cause of mockery for a clique of boys who made his life hell.

On his first Sunday home, a day of poignant pleasure and regret, he pleaded with Janey not to have to go back. It must have been heart-wrenching for her. Yes, I know, she said, but it'll get better with time. Things are never as bad as you think. Just wait a little longer and you'll get used to it...

The nightmares continued. Knowing her as he came to later, he thought that had it not been for Alexander she would have taken him away that first Sunday. She identified very closely with us, you know, and she hated to see either of us suffering emotionally...

Had he never been told, I asked, that I had been taken away from Pine-wood.

No, never. Perhaps Janey told you not to talk about it. If I had **known** I would certainly have used it. In fact, part way through my second term I virtually gave up importuning her because she seemed incapable of doing anything. I was no **happier** but I was beginning to resign myself. I felt that Alexander was blocking **her**.

And then one day a very kind woman arrived and asked me all sorts of questions. The experience disturbed me because I didn't know who or what she was. The next time I saw Janey she told me quite unexpectedly that I would be leaving school at the end of term. I couldn't believe it, even then didn't understand what had happened. Only years later, almost as a joke, Janey told me the woman was a child psychiatrist whom the school had called in without consulting her. She pronounced me perfectly normal but very highly strung. The headmaster sent Janey a letter suggesting that I be taken away because I was disturbing the others with my night-mares...

Life returned to normal again. For two or three terms Colin went to Hormel's. Janey cycled the twenty miles a day to accompany him both ways until she decided, from my experience perhaps, that something better was needed and found him a governess...

April 20

Colin left hurriedly after breakfast for Rome; his office at the UN Food and Agricultural Organization called him to a meeting which couldn't be postponed. Apologizing for the break in what was to have been three uninterrupted days together, he promised to be back by early evening.

I went out onto the terrace. My eyes wandered pleasurably over the green maze of vines ascending and descending the slopes and the soft blue hills beyond. Alexander, I recalled, was proud of Colin for having a recognizable job with the attendant salary and status in an international organization, and argued against his desire to leave it for a life tending his vines. In contrast, my nebulous occupations fitted none of Alexander's preconceived notions. His inability to find an acceptable definition of a life spent writing worried him. I heard his voice in the car on the way to the nursing home saying, once again, 'You're not idle all the time, are you, old boy?'

Janey, on the other hand viewed my constant scribbling with interest if not understanding. She knew me well enough to fear the worst, however, and made frequent attempts to forestall it, the last time only days before her death, I remember well. When you write a book, she pleaded, let it have a happy ending . . . I laughed. A happy ending seemed the last thing I expected of a book. But she insisted. And I remembered that as a child, when one had three wishes, she'd say one would be enough, because happiness included everything else. I reassured her as best I could and she lay back in bed seemingly content.

The calm of the sun-lit valley in front of me brought back memories of those warm Saturday summer afternoons Colin had spoken of, when Janey sat in her dungarees on the grass in the big field opposite Ron Jones's place watching us fly our planes. Perhaps she needed to rest, to get away for a few hours from the cares of wartime, perhaps she enjoyed the peaceful afternoon with us, I don't know I didn't think about it then; her presence was enough – a presence in those first war years constant enough to anchor me without being tied to her as in the past.

She liked Ron, we both liked him, and we were happy together. He liked her, too, I thought, as I went inside to fetch the transcripts, he seemed to enjoy coming down to the Manor, though I was so much younger than he that I could hardly have seemed much company. I leafed through the pages. Ah yes:-

The Manor was home from home for me then, it really was. A lovely old house with those low ceilings you could almost touch with your hand. Going through the back door and along the creaky passage and up the stairs to your bedroom – well, you see, I was really only used to cottage life, so it looked like the Lord of the Manor's place to me. Mother used to think the world of that house, didn't she? She always made me welcome whenever I came down. I used to go in and wander where I wanted. If you were having your dinner, I'd go upstairs on my own and wait for you to finish. Very often we played *Monopoly* with her or table tennis in the dining room. She used to really enjoy that. Just the three of us. She didn't have any company, it was all dark and desolate in the evenings with the blackout. And she wasn't very old then, was she? About thirty five, that's right. I wasn't at all reserved with her, although I was only a lad as you might say. I'd always call her Madam, unless we were playing a game and really getting into it, then we'd just speak naturally to one another. We were brought up to respect the gentry, taught to address them properly. Good morning, sir, you'd say, if you saw a gentleman in the village. The ladies weren't so important as I could understand. But the gentleman, yes. I think it's a good thing, too. Nowadays the kids have no respect for people and there isn't any gentry as there used to be . . .

—How often would you come down?

Every evening if I could. I was dead keen, there was nowhere at home for me to make these models, only out in the shed where there was no electric light. I made about ten models before I took a real interest, and then I purchased an exercise book and ruled it out with the date I started and finished each model, how much it cost me to make, how much I got for it if I sold it. Here's the book, look, you can have it if you like . . .

I looked through the battered notebook: in 1942 alone he had made fifty models, most of which he sold, I saw. It seemed as though he had been on a production line at the Manor. Ron laughed. He could finish a plane in a couple of evenings. He made a model of the King of Yugoslavia's personal plane, a Harvard, and it was presented to him. So they can't have been rough old things, can they? . . . No, that they weren't, I can see his hands to this day marking out the old bits of deal from his father's shop, holding them to the fretsaw, sanding, painting . . . But how had it all started, I asked.

Oh, you got interested in making models, and your mother must have said something to my father about me showing you how. I expect that was it. I had no real mate in the village then because I'd gone to school in Reading for two years until, at the start of the war, my father made an application for me to work for him because some of his workmen had been called up. That was another reason I enjoyed coming down. It was nice because you seemed to have an endless opportunity of having what you wanted. You had only to say to your mother and she went to Reading and brought it back, whatever it was . . .

—Surely you must have thought, here's this young whippersnapper who can have all these things and he doesn't know how to use them properly . . .

No. It wasn't as bad as that. I wasn't jealous. Until I knew you I didn't really know what it was to have more than what I had. We were brought up as country children with nothing. Neither my father nor mother were really bothered about us as children. My father never gave me a present in all my life. Your playroom was always loaded with stuff, but I didn't get jealous – never have done really. If you've got it, well the best of luck, that's what I say. Anyway, you seemed to mix in with me, didn't hold your head high and think, I'm the son of a lady and gentleman and you're one of the village rags, as you might put it. Of course, I wasn't in your category, I was only a village rough, but then you used to be dressed rough and ready like me. Mother didn't expect you to make models dressed up in a bow tie and Lord knows what. You were into everything, the same as me . . .

—But the age difference, all the same . . .

I don't remember a lot of difference between us. The main thing was we were dead keen on those aeroplanes, and I don't think we bothered with much else. You had no idea at all when you started, had you? But you did exceptionally well for a gentleman's son and not having the facility I had.

—You taught me everything I knew.

Well, it's like everything, you're brought up in a family, the father's a carpenter, the son's a carpenter. There are coffins laid in the churchyard which I made on my own and you couldn't tell the difference with ones my father made. And that was before I was called up at eighteen. If my father had given me an incentive to train I'd have been a first-class carpenter. But he was never interested, he just took me into his business – and learn yourself, that's it. And in the end I got out and became a lorry driver.

—There were other things we used to do together, do you remember? We went a bit wild with air-guns for a time. I hit you one day. I can still see you pulling your trouser-leg up very calmly and there was this hole with blood coming out. I was dead scared, but you got the slug out without seeming to bother much . . .

I don't remember. I know we used to get into trouble sometimes for ricocheting pellets off the house. Otherwise I don't think we used to get up to any mischief. Annie, if she ever saw us in a playful mood, would scream her head off. She used to think we were trying to catch her for Bert. He'd sit in the woodshed chopping firewood and tell us what to do. Get her out of the house, he'd say, keep her outside . . . And we'd go and lock the side door and as she went round to get in the back door he'd be waiting for her. If he was moving a bit quick, she'd scream at the top of her voice, Madam! Madam! and mother would come out and say, Don't chase her, Bert, or something like that. Nothing really happened about it. Bert was full of devilment, a jovial joker as you might say . . .

—Didn't you know he was having it off with her?

No. We were green then, only nippers. It wasn't like it is today. We knew she used to visit him pretty often, sometimes she'd come out to tease him when he was chopping wood, knowing full well that she'd get away before he could catch her. It was just a bit of devilment, really.

—I knew. I used to fancy having a go with her myself. Still, I haven't come here to talk about that! I wanted to ask why you refer to my mother as mother . . .

Because she used to treat me as one of hers almost, another son. She was always very nice, very pleasant to me. I never saw her upset, if ever anything went wrong she tried to make a joke of it. I liked her very much, I did, an exceptionally nice lady . . .

—And my father?

I don't remember much about him during the war. There were times perhaps when he came home on leave and you'd say, We'd better not do any modelling for a bit . . . And so I wouldn't come down to the Manor. But I remember him well out hunting before the war. All in black with his topper, and mother in a black bowler sitting beside him on her horse.

When I was a kid there were real country lords and ladies out hunting, not like nowadays when any old Dick or Harry can get on a horse. We used to go mad at school when the hunt came past, that was our delight. Times have changed completely, you don't realize now what village life was like before the war. Amnersfield was a small, close-knit community, the sons of the farm labourers were brought up to work on the farm and the daughters to go into service. There were almost as many gentry as village people, and we respected them. They ran fêtes, held flower shows, owned their own property, had cars and money. They had a better education, too, and they could help to broaden your outlook. As children we thought the world of these people. We didn't want their money, but we respected them for what they did for the village and for people who needed help. I mean, you couldn't very well go and ask them for help if you didn't respect them, could you? But all that came to an end, more or less, with the war, and I think it's a shame . . .

That afternoon at Colin's I re-discovered Lizzie, and she reminded me of those years when Ron had gone to war, leaving me bereft of a friend and companion. Before his departure I had noticed her only rarely playing with Colin or walking back from the village school, but I knew little of her existence otherwise, though only a few yards of corridor separated our rooms. I was surprised to learn the strength of her feelings for life at Amnersfield.

Oh, Ronnie, it was at the Manor that I came to life for the first time! Looking back, I feel I had no childhood before that time. I loved village life, loved to be able to wander through the fields at will, liked the people who were easy and friendly. At the Manor we lived in our own little community, our own world. Everything seemed so secure once we settled down . . .

Settling in at the village school, though, had been somewhat less than secure, she recalled. The other children called her a German, a Nazi and ostracised her. It was really tough, she was hurt and couldn't understand why they did it. She'd stand in a corner of the playground on her own, cut off from the others also by not knowing any of the rhymes and songs they sang or the games they played. At last, the headmaster called the children together under the chestnut tree and explained to them that Lizzie had been thrown out of her country by the Nazis, that her father was in India and that they weren't to call her a Nazi. The headmaster's authority was sufficient to win the day and thereafter she not only enjoyed the school but became one of its star pupils.

Had they made anything of her being Jewish, I asked.

No, she said, but that was perhaps because she had never felt Jewish herself. Her parents weren't practising Jews and she felt that they had been forced to leave Austria for no other reason than that they weren't wanted there. She shut that part of her life off completely, she didn't want anything more to do with Vienna.

I felt at home in England, it was like heaven to me. The doors were open and people took me as I was. It was simple village life. The school children were probably only repeating what their parents said at home, repeating propaganda. They didn't really know what was going on. Whereas every time I closed my eyes I could hear the sound of marching boots. It still frightens me. But I wasn't frightened at Amnersfield, it seemed like one big happy family . . .

—Even though you were excluded from the nursery and other places in the house?

Oh, but that didn't last very long. One day, after Annie had left, your mother called me in to play with Colin. It was an honour, Ronnie, I really felt that. There was I, a 'bloody foreigner' allowed to go into the nursery, an Aladdin's cave full of books and toys and games that I could touch instead of just look at! And then, because your mother insisted that Colin had to be outdoors so many hours of the day, we started to play in the garden on our bikes, snow-balling, collecting conkers. I felt protective towards him, I wouldn't say I wanted to mother him but I felt he needed love and I gave him what I could . . .

—Why? Did you feel he lacked his mother's love?

Maybe. She loved him, gave him everything under the sun, but whether he actually had a mother's love, I don't know. She was very good and kind, she treated me as one of the family which is something I shan't ever forget, but she seemed terribly withdrawn. I can't remember her getting down on the floor to play with us. She'd stand at the nursery door to watch instead. When we used to cycle down to the weir to swim she'd laugh and joke with us, but underneath she always seemed far away in a world of her own. She wasn't involved somehow in our world . . .

Lizzie remembered her as a lonely figure-head, a great lady. After dinner,

Janey would ring a little hand-bell to announce that she was leaving the dining room and sometimes she stopped at the door to thank them for the meal. Then she'd wave her hand, with the coloured nail polish that fascinated Lizzie, and vanish like a queen in her blue evening dress into the smoking room. Sometimes when Lizzie took in her coffee she'd find her kneeling on the floor reading in front of the fire. Alone, lonely . . .

Lizzie's special treat was to be asked to have tea with Janey and Colin in the garden. Otherwise, of course, I never ate with you. I wasn't born to be a cook's daughter, I know, but that was the lot life gave me. I knew my place. Yet I never felt that she treated me like that. One day I was going up the front stairs and when I was half way up I stopped, horrified. Your mother was at the top and must have seen my change of expression because she said, What's happened? . . . Do you realize, Madam, that I was coming up to help you but I've used the front stairs. I am sorry . . . Don't be silly, she replied, from now on you can use them all the time . . .

—Did you always call her Madam?

Yes, of course. It was engrained in me. Madam was Madam and you were master Ronnie . . . You know, when you came here to my house the other day I said to my husband, Shall I call him master Ronnie or not? . . . He said, Don't be silly . . . But I couldn't help it. We became firm friends, played together, but I knew you were the son of the house. I didn't feel inferior to you because of it and you never made me feel as though I were. Yet there was always that dividing line . . .

At the start, she went on, it had been much easier for her to get on with Colin than with me. He needed love and accepted what she could give him. Whereas you, Ronnie, had been more drilled and knew class distinctions better. But after Ron Jones left for the air force, we became closer. I used to help you with your models, you read books to me, taught me ping-pong and tennis. You were always nice to me, you shared all your books and games, and we spent hours together. Do you remember sitting at the top of the tower room stairs, talking about I don't know what? You were still at school and I was already working as an apprentice alteration hand in a Reading store where your mother had arranged for me to be trained. I don't know what we had in common to talk about, but we spent hours up there.

—Ah yes! How did we become sexually involved at that early age? Do you remember?

I don't know, I think it started off, I was friendly with Colin and you were just the elder son of the house and you became involved in playing with us. You came into the nursery one day and saw Colin and me playing with something and you said, Do it this way . . . and you took over as leader. We followed whatever you said. You got extremely cross with Colin for upsetting something in your room and banished him. He was heart-broken and cried for days, he was very frightened of you. You were very strict, I don't remember hearing you laugh much at the beginning. But later you changed, you were awfully good to me. The only time you did something I didn't like was when a young girl came to the Manor to go riding on your pony and you'd tell me to go away. You had no time for me then. I couldn't understand why. It sticks in my mind because usually you were very kind. I was jealous of her, I suppose . . .

—It sounds very unkind. I don't remember it. It was at a time when you and I were having our first sexual explorations, wasn't it?

Yes, we were, to be honest.

—How do you recall it happening?

I don't know, I never thought about it. I don't know if other kids did it or not. I don't know, there's no doubt those were happy times at the Manor, a marvellous life. As I say, I came to life there, no doubt about it . . .

As I heard Colin's car coming down the drive I was still remembering the embarrassment of that final part of the conversation with Lizzie whom I hadn't seen for thirty years (in which time she had made a successful career as fashion seamstress for British royalty). There were shared memories we could no longer share. It was with some relief that we ended the interview and sat down to Cookie's excellent apfelstrudel and chatted about other things . . .

Colin came in looking tired and suggested a stroll. In silence, we walked down the rows of vines in the evening sunlight, feeling the heat still rising from the earth. There was something pleasing in the shared silence, a closeness we had missed in our lives. I was reflecting on Janey's distance, which Lizzie remembered so well when, unexpectedly, Colin stopped. For a moment I thought his attention had been caught by some office or vineyard problem and I waited. Then in a strained, almost painful voice, he said: You know, there's one thing I've never said to anyone. It came to me in the car driving back. When Janey died I felt a sense of liberation, of elation almost. I walked for a long time up the river thinking that finally I was free. I was twenty-one and yet, you know, I can't remember her funeral. And now I often dream that she's a shadowy figure who didn't die after all . . .

I put my arm around him. I felt exactly the same . . . He looked at me with surprise. Yes, it was her death that freed me to start a new life in Spain. There are so many things we share which we've never talked about. Only I don't dream about her. I live a deep yearning for what might have been.

I didn't know, he said. I thought we were so different. You were always so distant. Perhaps it was the five years between us . . .

Probably. Or perhaps we both wanted the same . . . As we reached the terrace and sat down, I went on: After all this, she eludes me still. I have an impression of her that perhaps you can't share. It comes from something mysterious in her that made me believe she was a miracle-worker—

Who could rescue you if she wanted? That's very much how I felt! And it was often true. She could solve the problems I faced – only looking back, I can see that they weren't the real problems. Avoiding conflict at all costs, she couldn't solve these . . .

No. But why did she seem at once elusive and inescapable, so that only her death released us in some way, I asked.

He reflected for a moment. Inescapable, I think, because beyond any shadow of doubt, she seemed the person who was going to solve everything. Even in adolescence I still felt it. Elusive, perhaps because of her unauthoritative manner. She didn't seemingly try to control our lives, she avoided conflict, as I've said. Her control through the emotions was much more subtle. Hurt was a word she used very often. It hurts me very much when you do that . . .

Her ability to pass on this feeling produced an emotional stress in him, a sense of guilt and depression. It was much more effective than straight anger and a good telling off. For hours he'd be depressed, fearing that he had lost her affection, until she'd say, All right, now let's forget about it . . . The feeling had stayed with him throughout life.

Yes, I said, I'd forgotten the way she used hurt, or rather the threat of

losing her love. I've been through this with the analyst, too, and he
believes . . . It was the first time I had mentioned some of the things P. has
said. But, I went on, I still feel that P. fails to grasp that she lacked an essential core. She had no defined personality that I could come to grips with.

Except on some minor things, she held no strong convictions, Colin
agreed. Her horizons beyond county life came from her travels, not
intellectual pursuits. Books, art and music were rarely, if ever, discussed;
politics was not a matter of conversation, for one was conservative and that
was that. Socialism was an abhorrent, pejorative word. Bored by serious
newspapers she read the *Daily Express* to Alexander's dismay. Minor dis-
tastes, on the other hand, were forcefully expressed. She disliked baroque
music, Bach especially, detested fishing, believing that if it was easier to
catch a fish with a worm than a fly, the former should be preferred, was
fearful of bats, convinced that they would get tangled in her hair, hated
snakes and had a loathing of cooked English breakfasts, particularly
porridge. She told a joke about a Frenchman who, feeling sick in rough
weather on a Channel ferry, struggled into the restaurant to find a Scot in
good form with a plate of porridge in front of him. Excuse me, monsieur, the
Frenchman said, are you about to eat or have you eaten that?

I laughed, remembering the joke, and remembering also that her convictions on matters more important than porridge had on occasion been
forcefully expressed. But before I could comment, Colin continued:

There was a curious mixture of rationality and irrationality in her, you
know. Do you remember her faith in planchette? We spent hours in front
of that little heart-shaped board on wheels with a pencil stuck through it on
which each of us placed a hand. It was uncanny, it never moved across the
big sheets of brown paper laid on the table under it until we asked a question. And then it would trace out either Yes or No. The Yes always
finished with a big upward flourish, the No with a downsweep. Janey
would tell me that in the past it had predicted certain things for her that
had come true. Her seriousness about it strongly influenced me, would do
so even today. We took turns to ask it questions, mainly about the future.
Many of them, I remember, were coloured by Janey's desire for happiness
or the idea that happiness was the major aim in life. It was her over-riding
preoccupation. She'd ask questions about Alexander – would he be posted
to X, would he be coming home soon . . . I used to be pleased at that sort of
question because I had very ambivalent feelings about him returning on
leave . . .

Well, I said, I found the whole business of planchette slightly sinister. Who was supposed to be answering the questions? Or was she pushing the board? I didn't like it. But you've reminded me of something equally irrational but more harmful. She had an aversion to my wearing glasses that nearly crippled me as a kid. For most of my time at Hormel's and my first couple of terms at public school, I couldn't see the blackboard. Knowing her hostility to glasses, I was ashamed to tell her. Instead, I had a small telescope, three or four inches long, which she had given me and which I could hide in the palm of my hand. I'd sit in class with my hand against one eye squinting at the blackboard, which even then I couldn't always see, and pretending that everything was normal. Why no one ever said anything I can't imagine.

I didn't know about the telescope. It must have been after she took us to that quack doctor to do eye exercises, wasn't it? As far as I was concerned, exercises were a total waste of time because I suffer from astigmatism, but she didn't take me to an optician to find out. I was nineteen, perhaps twenty before I wore glasses because Janey believed that they were some sort of weakness . . .

And the telescope a strength, I put in . . . He looked at me in surprise. Yes, well this will sound bizarre, no doubt – wait a minute, I'll get my notebook. Perhaps this might make some sense . . . I pointed to the page as he took the book.

June 9, 1981

' . . . I've always thought that my sense of liberation during the war came from a new social freedom alone. But I'm beginning to think that it had also to do with a growing independence of my mother, who let me develop an "I" that seemed my own . . . '

Silence.

Out of the blue comes a memory as clear as yesterday. 'She gave me an "I" – an e-y-e – once.'

'How do you mean?'

'Surely I must have told you? The telescope? No?' Briefly I explain. 'It's curious that no one ever noticed at school . . . '

'No one noticed, eh? Well, why didn't you do something if you couldn't see properly?' It's the first time he has openly expostulated at my failure to take my life in my own hands.

'Yes, of course. Protest to my mother! Demand glasses! But you see, she had firm views on the matter. Perhaps I was frightened to tell her that those stupid eye exercises had done no good. She had just rescued me from boarding school and I felt I could ask no more of her . . . '

'So she rescued you again by giving you a telescope-penis to carry round like Nelson.'

I burst out laughing. 'She considered glasses a weakness, yes, though she wore them herself for reading. I always thought it was because my father wore glasses.'

'It sounds like vanity to me.'

'Probably. Well, there's no point in worrying about that now.'

'But she colluded with you. She gave you a telescope-penis to overcome your weakness . . . '

'She gave me a telescope, yes. I think it gave me a feeling of being special, different . . . ' As I say it, a familiar and debilitating sense of separateness overwhelms me. Other people seem to swim in the world, I thought this morning; their inner and outer realities flow into each other, separate but connected, like the water that was flowing round and holding me up as I splashed along my daily half-mile swim. But inside my head I was standing as always at the edge of the pool.

'Why do you think you need to feel special?'

'To compensate for not feeling special, for a sense of powerlessness, I suppose . . . But don't all children want to feel special, to their parents at least?'

'Of course. But they come to learn slowly that they're not as special as perhaps they wanted to imagine.'

'Why didn't I?'

Silence. He shifts in the chair behind me. 'You didn't go through the process of gradual disillusionment about your mother that children have to go through.'

'I don't really understand.'

Well, he said, an infant had to go through a process of separation from its mother, didn't it? In a first stage, of becoming aware that the breast wasn't an extension of itself which, like magic, satisfied its desires. An original state of bliss, a Garden of Eden from which we were all banished. As it became increasingly aware of the mother as a separate and autonomous being, of a reality in which others existed and desires weren't magically satisfied, so its sense of self developed, ego boundaries became drawn between the 'me' and the 'not-me' and the infant established a sense of autonomy. 'It's a long voyage of disillusionment from a magical to a real world,' he concluded.

'And you're saying that I never arrived . . .'

'Some of the yearning for the magic has remained, hasn't it? Your mother flitting in and out of your life didn't help. Sometimes you must have phantasized that you could magically, omnipotently summon her up, at other times you felt powerless . . .'

'So I never came to grips with reality, hers or mine? That's probably true.'

There's a long silence. Then I say: 'Is that what you mean by her collusion?'

'Yes.'

'You think she should have left me at boarding school, for example?'

'It might have been better to let you follow your father's route. You might have found fuller independence in the end, broken with his *mores* just the same but later.'

'Intellectually, I might agree. But emotionally I'll never feel that. I've never regretted her decision, just as I promised her.'

'But exactly. It was collusive of her to make you swear never to resent her for doing it. Just as it was collusive of her to ''save'' you again by giving you a telescope instead of getting you glasses. Her demands on you were sometimes mischievous, perverse . . .'

I'm silenced. For what seems an eternity I lie hoping that the session will end and I won't have to admit to the guilty sensation of pleasure flowing like warm water through me. A rational remark comes to my defence: 'Well, it proves what I've always thought. The Oedipal complex isn't a one-way affair . . .'

' . . .'

'All right. You said the telescope was a penis. What did you mean?'

'It depends on what it meant to you both. I don't know.'

'I can't say what it meant to my mother, I could only speculate. As far as I'm concerned it means nothing.'

' . . .'

'I suppose I'm refusing to recognize something . . .' His sudden silences irritate me after his unaccustomed forthcomingness. 'Well, it was your suggestion,' I say.

'The penis perhaps that would compensate for yours which was smaller than you father's . . .'

'I suppose I wanted to be the master, is that it?'

'Yes . . . Well, we'll have to leave it there for today.'

Colin handed the notebook back. I don't know what to make of the telescope interpretation, he said. Sounds very Freudian. But Janey's collusion certainly rings true.

It's not only her collusion, it was my need – no, demand, I'd say – for it.

I'm sure I felt the same. As the what's his name, analyst, says, we wanted that magical part of her. It explains something about our seeing her as a miracle-worker, and also, perhaps, why it was so difficult to break from her.

Do you remember what she used to say: The road to hell is paved with good intentions... Well, it wasn't hell, just paradise lost.

She wanted to be much closer to you, you know, he said.

Really?

Yes. But she could never understand you. She used to talk to me abut it. She'd suggest going to the cinema, for example, and you'd reply, Mmm, I suppose so... Your lack of enthusiasm irritated her so intensely that she'd go, Aaargh!... She could never get at you, never grasp your essence. I was much easier because I was more outgoing, enthusiastic. But you were unreachable, like Alexander, she used to say. Just as he disappeared behind the *Times* and grunted at her, you disappeared behind an inscrutable lack of reaction to anything. It was a characteristic she disliked deeply in both of you, and it destroyed something in her, I believe – the will to communicate with you...

I don't remember being as bad as that, I said.

Oh, you were! Sometimes I'd hear her ask if you were depressed. It was a word she used quite often about herself though I don't recall her ever appearing depressed. But you'd reply, No... in a depressed tone. You were withdrawn, emotionally dead. Always on the defensive, warding off questions, not letting her get in to you. You'd never say directly what you felt. Janey thought it was something you'd inherited from Alexander...

But Betty, Lizzie, even Bert give a different picture, I objected. And I remember being happy...

You didn't give that appearance. The only time you seemed open was with Ron Jones, he brought you out. With me you were generally moody or uninterested, as I mentioned when I told you about shooting Joyce in the leg. Sometimes I could just chatter on and it was all right with you, but most of the time you'd tell me to bugger off in a moody voice.

But didn't we sometimes play together?

If there was no one else. You invented a game of tag on bikes and another of stalking each other in the dark with those powerful torches Janey gave us one Christmas. If you were 'shot' by the other's beam you were dead. But most of the time you were distant, almost a stranger, and that's how you remained throughout my adolescence and early adulthood. You showed no warmth towards me, never comforted me . . .

Yes, I know, I lived with the shutters down on you and Janey. In analysis it came to me once that your arrival meant a rival for my little bit of paradise or Garden of Eden, as P. says. It's a strange experience to discover these fragments of a hidden script beneath the story of one's life — hieroglyphs inscribed on broken shards that have to be pieced together and interpreted. I wish we had been able to start on this sooner.

Yes, well there's still time. I know we haven't finished but I'm exhausted now. I'd love you to stay on a day or two longer, but you know the air-traffic controllers are going on strike the day after tomorrow . . .

April 21

One of those Mediterranean spring mornings when, under a shimmering sky, the earth appears refreshed and warm with anticipation, brought Colin back, it seemed, to memories of hours lost in contemplation of sky and cloud, freedom and space, at the top of the tall chestnut by the Manor's back gate; memories of lying in bed listening to the wind in the branches of the pine outside his bedroom and dreaming of wandering over the countryside at will. It was the last year of the war, and Georgie Wills, oldest son of an evacuee family Janey had recently moved from the hostel to Mrs. Winteringham's cottage, had become his constant companion. Together they roamed the fields and hedgerows without thought or preoccupation, he recalled.

Absorbed by the calm that such mornings and memories bring, we drove through the wooded green hills on the road to Rome. You know, he said, breaking the silence, I often long to return to that last year of the war . . .

Surprised, I waited for him to continue.

There's nothing strange about it, I suppose. I was totally free of the pressures and conflicts people create in me. I'll do anything, to the point of deviousness, to avoid conflict.

Like Janey, I said.

I get it from her, he replied. She was like blotting paper, absorbing conflict from all sides to ensure an appearance of harmony. It means that very often I feel I'm playing a role, I'm not myself.

Our family couldn't handle aggression, I said. It was either Alexander's violent outbursts or Janey's blotting paper. But the role wasn't limited to that, was it?

No, certainly. Even during the war that sense of being socially different never totally vanished, did it? We always had a role to play, an image to project, which meant not expressing some very real feelings. I probably escaped more lightly than you, though...

I always imagined you had. You escaped Alexander. Inadequacy isn't one of your basic feelings, perhaps.

No, insecurity rather, he replied. Like Alexander. I have an affection for him now, I'm concerned about him in the nursing home...

Yes, I said, remembering the moment of leaving him alone in the strange room... It felt as though I were disposing of him. All he wanted was to die...

It must have been very painful, Colin said. I'm planning to go to England soon to see him. There are lots of things about him that I appreciate, but almost as many that I dislike. His exaggerated concern with the world's opinion, his fear of conflictive truths, his intolerance of criticism. Yet I share these traits, feel doomed to be like him.

I know that feeling, I replied. He's where we don't want him – inside us. I paused. I'm surprised that the last year of the war was a happy time for you...

Ah, he said, glancing at me. I suppose you felt it more, didn't you? At the start I did, too, but then...

Yes... I turned on the tape-recorder, hoping that the car's sound wouldn't drown his words. Tell me what you remember...

I

'While staying with my brother I had a dream. I was in a room separated from another by a narrow passage. Outside, the night sky was suddenly filled with planes in combat. As I struggled to shut the window there was a loud crash in the other room. A pilot, evidently wounded or shocked, appeared and I went across to comfort him. As he turned his face to me, I returned, still solicitous, to the other room. In the corridor, a woman stood silently watching . . .'

What are my associations, he asks as always.

The part about the pilot seemed fairly obvious, I replied. 'Another crash . . . But my first thought when I awoke was not of him. It was of East and West: the rooms were cardinally opposite each other. It seemed that they were the polarities at war with each other in myself . . .'

He makes no comment for a long time. Then: 'East and West — could that be your father and mother?'

'Yes. Or my mother and Ilse. Do they have to be exclusive?'

'No.'

'Perhaps, like Colin, my world collapsed at the beginning of the war with Ilse's and Alexander's departure.'

'Well, they were East and West, weren't they? On enemy sides . . .'

'Yes, it's true. I hadn't thought of that. But even more unsettling was not knowing which side my mother was on. For a time, you know, I thought she was a spy . . . It seemed like a continuation of all her other ambiguities . . .'

During the silence, as I feel again the frightening exhilaration of uncertainty, an urgent desire to urinate comes over me. To distract myself, I relate my surprise at the range of feelings Colin and I share.

'Although there were differences,' I add. 'He used to wake every night and – ' Floating off the back wall of my mind a memory forces its way through the words and I find myself saying that, after my return from Pinewood, I would often wake in the middle of the night and be unable to find the door to get to the bathroom. 'Although I'd slept in that room half my life by then, it was as though I were shut up in a dark box and couldn't see my way out. It must have coincided with the eye exercises . . .'

'Couldn't see physically or metaphorically?'

'Both, I suppose.'

'And what would it have been that you didn't want to see at night? Who your mother was with?'

'No, no, it was before that . . . It had to do with her being a spy.'

'So you didn't want to see for fear of what you might find out about her.'

'As a spy she'd be betraying us, wouldn't she?'

'Betraying your father especially, you might have felt then.'

'Ah! . . .' Out there, in the corridor beyond the bedroom, there's a darkness so intensely black and threatening that in my mind I recoil from it. Who or what do I fear meeting out there? My mother in a hidden role? The darkness seems totally taken up by her menacing presence. 'I feel I must be projecting my hostility onto her,' I say. 'She's like a witch waiting to annihilate me with a terrifying curse for having unwittingly caught her out . . .'

'The other side of the fairy godmother who had just rescued you from boarding school . . .'

'Mmm . . . I've never seen this side of her before . . . The rescue hadn't brought us much closer together, my brother talks of the way I shut her out of my life. I'd hoped, I suppose, that rescue meant she had chosen me as the man of the house. Instead, I found that I was just a schoolboy who couldn't cope . . .'

'And so you saw her as an enemy witch who refused you that bedroom which the fairy godmother seemed to offer . . .'

'Yes. And I only wanted to see one side . . .' In her long evening dress, once, in the smoking room, I touched her, felt her body under the silky material. Only for a moment, only that once. I'd started to wrestle with her – was that it? Yes, and when my arms met the firmness of her body a sense of amazement made me recoil. Or was it not rather guilt? Who was I to her? Sometimes, sitting close by the fire, she would talk to me as though I were a man. And at other, more important times, she told me nothing . . .

'...'

I fell silent, too, pervaded by a redolence, a musty warmth that soothed and comforted the inner emptiness. Was it just adolescence, growing up? Not only. It was coming out of isolation, emerging into a world of human warmth, sensuality, touches shared. There were the long hours Ron and I spent on our own, absorbed in the models we were making. Sometimes, as though the tension were too great, we would wrestle each other to the floor and then, from displays of strength to tenderness, caress the other to orgasm. 'It was something which we openly accepted, without making anything of, as part of the bond between us...'

He makes no comment.

'And then there were the sexual gropings with Lizzie on the tower room stairs, in the hay-loft, out in the playhouse... And when I talked to Bert in the woodshed he'd give me advice, one of the few times he answered my questions more or less seriously...'

Well, I had to try to put you on the right path, didn't want you making a fool of yourself. Scraping away at that all bloody night and then being ill the next day. Or cluttering up the Manor House with young Jews or cross-breeds and all that...

The long silence is broken at last by him saying, 'You seem to have left the dream behind. The comings and goings from the room – are those your mother's?'

'It doesn't fit somehow...' Then I see the corridor outside the guest bedroom along which I cautiously tread in the night so as not to be heard, wanting not to hear and yet fascinated by what I heard.

'All the same, the pilot...' he suggests.

'Yes, I know. And the worst part of it was that I didn't see it coming...' Resentment wells up like an ulcerous vapour. 'It's when I'm confident that the crashes happen. I was blind. Bert saw it and never warned me. From the start he didn't like the looks of the Wing Commander, I was re-reading it last night...'

A cocky little bugger, he seemed to me. He'd come bouncing along, I'm it, sort of thing. I remember the day we was milking and your mother said she had to have the air force billeted on her and she didn't want them. There was nothing she could do, though, and soon two officers came. It wasn't long before Leroy weeded the other one out so he could be there alone...

And for a long time Madam keeps to herself and one day I say to her, I've twice to serve, twice to wash up. Could you not arrange that I cook all the meals together? . . . All right, Cookie, she said, I don't like it but if you think . . . And then the Wing Commander come in the kitchen and I say to myself, he's a nice fellow. He was sitting at the kitchen table and he told me his story. I tell him Madam promised me meals are together now. Yes? he said. So he changed to a dinner jacket. And I say to Madam, he's ever so nice a man . . . And she laughed. She was beautiful. I couldn't believe it myself. So lonely . . .

P. says nothing.
'And I asked Bert and Cookie when they had first noticed . . . '

I soon saw, Ronnie, what his game was. Dr Rogers was up home one day and we saw Leroy coming over the lawn with your mother. My God, that's Leroy, isn't it? old Rogers said . . . Yes, he's billeted here . . . Fancy that, Bert, he said, he was billeted on me and I got him out . . .

—Why was that?

He'd been causing trouble with his missus. He's a bloody trouble-maker, he said, I bloody soon had him out . . . Well, hearing that . . .

Oh, Ronnie, she needed more attention, more life. When your father is coming home he's more interested in getting the fire to light than in her. And one morning I look at Madam and I say, You look so happy today . . . Do you think so, Cookie? she said . . . Yes, you look it . . . I think I am, she said and went out . . . Madam knew she could trust me with everything. As a woman, I was thinking how happy she must be . . .

At first, I felt that his presence was taking Janey away from me again. But I came to like him because he was full of stories that appealed to a kid. His childhood in New Zealand, his escape from France in 1940, the famous fighter squadrons he'd served in before the war. And then, too, he wore pilot's wings which fascinated me . . .

'I shared Colin's feelings,' I said to P. 'He seemed a breath of fresh air. He was an outsider who derided county values. For him, riding was gaucho-style, fishing was deep-sea for marlin and shark. But it was his dream which won me over. He was going to buy a Dutch barge and sail round the world after the war. It seemed like a projection of wartime liberation into the post-war . . . '

'He was becoming, perhaps, a model for the father you missed . . . '

'Yes. Although he was, I thought, only a friendly, temporary presence. None the less, he was fun . . . '

Oh, we had to laugh at the things he did. He must get round Madam because he was so humorous. On her birthday he picked flowers from the garden – your own garden – and in the middle he put a big onion, and he sent up this bouquet to her bedroom with a beautiful ribbon. He was very human, you had to like him . . .

Full of practical jokes which, as a kid, I thought were wonderful. He plotted with me once to let a piglet loose in the dining room as he and Janey sat down to lunch. It scampered in, just as we'd planned, and slithered round on the polished floor. He and I thought it hilarious. Janey wasn't that amused, as I recall . . .

Oh, but she laughed all right when he put the pony in the smoking room and I had to tell her there was an important visitor waiting. You'll clean up, Mary, won't you? The Wing Commander said to me beforehand . . .

'He took me seriously, you see, he'd discuss his plans for writing a book with me. He'd known Hilary, the Battle of Britain hero whose book was all the rage. I encouraged him, excited by the prospect of knowing a writer at last. He bought sheaves of thick, luscious cream paper, some pre-war stock he found somewhere, got hold of a typewriter and closetted himself in the drawing room with a WRAF secretary . . . '

P. says nothing.

And from the kitchen I hear your mother and him laughing over dinner, laughing happy when they go to the smoking room. I can't say how happy she was. I knew exactly what was going on. I felt proud, guilty of being a match-maker . . .

Walking round the garden with her, coming up to the cowshed when she and I were milking, taking her out in the car. The bastard, I said to the missus . . .

Once he took us down to Weymouth to look for a Dutch barge. From the hotel on the sea-front we watched American landing craft practising for D-Day. I remember the jeeps being driven off them and almost disappearing into the sea, their drivers standing up in vests and underpants in the freezing cold. But there weren't any Dutch barges . . .

'After a couple of Saturday afternoons spent dictating, his book was suddenly forgotten. Perhaps the sun shone and it was a good day for an outing. There was no time like the present for organizing pleasure, it soon became apparent . . . '

And then one day your father arrived in a car. And I am thinking, what shall I say to him? Madam had been away some time. Where's my wife? he said, coming into the kitchen . . . She'll come a bit later, I said, I'll make your meal if you want . . . No, I'll wait . . . And then Madam comes in with the Wing Commander in a car, comes into the kitchen very excited. She was wearing the Wing Commander's coat. Madam, I say, your husband is coming in . . . Is he? She was shaking. She ask if I had told him where she had been and I say, No . . . Then she go out. The next morning when your father went away she was changed, very serious. And I was thinking, What's going to happen now? . . .

'I must have started to shut out certain areas of feeling by then. I remember one afternoon a boy ran up at Hormel's school and said he had just seen my mother with an RAF officer in town. "Was that your father?" Something cracked but I covered up. A couple of nights later, going to the bathroom to pee, I heard her voice in the Wing Commander's room. I crept by so silently that they didn't hear and shut myself up with a feeling of having done a great wrong . . . '

'It made you aware of her availability to men,' he says.

'Patently,' I reply with an edge in my voice.

The same edge Mary said she heard when I contradicted her. ''Mummy hasn't gone to London for the day, she's gone to Oxford for the night . . . '' As you said it, you looked at me a bit queer. But you weren't the sort to show your worries openly, you kept them to yourself . . .

—You knew by then, I suppose.

Yes. Strictly between you and me, I remember making his bed one morning and finding some curlers. Do you use these in your hair now? I asked, and he laughed. Yes, I do . . . He wasn't embarrassed. You could talk to him like that, he treated you like a friend. I liked him, he was a jolly, joking sort of chap, always full of beans. But I wouldn't have said a word about it all. Your mother was always so good to me that I was absolutely loyal. You're the only one I've ever talked to about it . . .

'Yes, but what I meant about availability was something else,' P. says. 'Perhaps if you had felt a stronger attachment between your father and mother you'd have accepted her unavailability to you more easily . . .'

'Are you saying that I wanted to see my parents divided so that I could imagine prising her away from him?'

'That may have been what you wanted but also feared.'

'Feared? His revenge, you mean. Maybe. But at that moment I could see what was coming and tried to pretend it wasn't. The split again. And when it came I was caught singularly off guard . . .'

Silence. Why repeat it yet again?

'Yes,' he says sympathetically. 'Well, we'll have to leave it there for today.'

May 5

Silence.

'What are you thinking about?' he asks at last.

'Something you said not long ago . . . Triumphing over trauma.'

' . . .'

'I didn't believe it when you said it, but it feels right now. That's why I haven't been able to write the book.'

'I don't follow you.'

'No? Didn't I use to talk about disposing of the past? Of wanting to rub it out and, at the same time, preserve it?'

'Yes.'

'The aims seem contradictory, don't they? But they're the same. I kept the past alive out of a desire for revenge. One day I would write it – and *them* – off the face of the earth . . .'

I hear his feet shuffle behind my head, the rustle of his trousers as his legs cross, and I realize that there is nothing new in my words.

'It's what you tried to do with your mother, isn't it? Blot her out.'

'To shut out the pain and take revenge . . . Yes.' After a pause I add: 'Wasn't it what we were saying only a couple of months ago? It shows how we just go round and round, passing the same point again and again

from a different angle. Like the chess story – how many times have I
related it? It comes to mind again, I don't know why . . . We were alone
once more. Leroy had left for France soon after D-Day. Perhaps I hoped he
had gone for good, perhaps it was finding myself the man of the house
again after my first term at public school, I don't know, but my guard was
down. I was quite unprepared, yes, unsuspecting when one evening
during a game of chess – a game I had taught her – she looked up and said:
"I think you should know, darling, Wing Commander Leroy and I are
going to be married." I saw her flush with confusion. My face grew hot. It
was a moment of intenseness and I felt immediately that she needed my
help, my acquiescent approval. I looked at the chessboard, my hand still
touching the pawn with which I had countered her last move, and
suddenly I knew I had nothing to say. I had lost.

' "It's your move," I murmured.

' "Oh, you're more interested in who's going to win this game, aren't
you?" And she put out a hand and moved a piece at random. I wanted to
cry, "No!" but I couldn't. The truth was too big to tell. The channel
along which communication had flowed was cut off at that moment. We
couldn't understand each other. I'd keep silent in future. There wasn't
anything I wanted to say. And that's how it remained until the end of her
life.'

'Well, as we've said before, you used the chess as a defence. In rejecting
her you were defending yourself.'

'Of course. Bringing the shutters down.'

'But her answer,' he continues, 'was also self-defensive.'

'Yes.' I see with surprise that my remark about it being her move had
another meaning. 'It was her responsibility, her choice what she did.'

'A choice about which you could do nothing.'

'And so I cut her out. And that was the end . . . '

In the back of my mind I hear Colin again. He didn't understand. What
did it mean? . . . It means that daddy and I won't be married any
more . . . He panicked. Alexander was no longer going to be there. Not
even as the hovering background presence he had become . . . No, she
said, Alexander would still be his daddy, but she was going to marry
Leroy . . . The whole thing was a total surprise. Once I got over the shock I
wasn't unhappy because I liked Leroy, but I was worried enough to want
to talk to you about it. I tried, but you wouldn't say anything, you just
gave non-committal, intimidating answers . . .

And I could have knocked him bloody flat. He bounced up to the cow-shed one day and told me outright they were going to be married and he'd be in charge of everything. After that, his word was law, your mother agreed with everything he said. It wasn't like a family any more. Admittedly, he'd talk to me more than your father would, he was a jolly little bugger in that, but it didn't make me like him any the better. He wasn't gentry, he just jumped into a good thing. I said to the missus, that bastard's going to have every halfpenny out of her, you see. And I still believe that if he hadn't ever come, your mother and father would be at the Manor House now . . .

That was the end. I come down one morning and all the carpets are rolled up and there are labels on them, on the chairs and pictures saying they belong to your father. He was home, the Wing Commander was in the invasion. What's happening here? I say . . . and Madam explained. Your father was leaving, taking all his things. It was only a short time before I left. I get a letter from my husband in India, he has me and Lisel on the priority list for a ship. Madam comes into the kitchen and I tell her . . . You can't go, she says . . . I must, or my marriage will break up . . . So I just made up my mind and we left.

'So that was how it all ended at the Manor . . . After that it was a perpetual flight — Switzerland, Canada, Switzerland again — well, I've told you . . . Janey and Leroy never settled. Colin and I followed them round.

'The end at the Manor — but not of the illusion,' P. says after a time.

'About my mother? She wasn't an illusion. My childhood was spent struggling painfully in search of her.'

'That's part of the human condition, isn't it? To seek the unattainable. In art, writing . . .'

'You mean, I should have accepted the inevitable. Spared myself the only desire that gave meaning to childhood?' Again, in the dressing room where she's packing to leave, I watch as the lid of the large box she's bringing down falls off to reveal a wedding dress. She smiles enigmatically at me without a word and closes the box . . .

'You wanted her totally, didn't you?'

'Yes.' I'm silent. 'It was unacceptable, I was wrong. And yet I've always refused to admit it.'

'She didn't help you as much as she might,' he says quietly.

'No, perhaps not. She was wrong too, it wasn't her fault. She loved too much . . .'

'...'

'A perverse love, you once said. A transgression, I think. I followed her enchanted way instead of my father's socially accepted path. But I never found her waiting at the end of it. It's been a struggle ever since.'

'Uh-huh...'

'But it was her way I wanted and go on wanting...' I feel, more than hear, the thought rising from somewhere and I hold it to myself until at last I hear my voice say: 'I wanted to love, not destroy her...' And then the silence closes in again.

May 11

'I've reached the bottom line: to accept the destruction and start again...'

In the inner darkness I look across the years in silence, waiting until I hear him say:

'Without accepting it you wouldn't find parts of the lost ones in you again. It's like mourning...'

'Mourning, yes...'

I laid down the notebook and looked desolately out of the window. 'I didn't feel anything,' I hear myself say again.

P. was silent; I don't think he believed it.

'It was as though an old man, whom I cared for because he was old and helpless, had died. A fortunate death, without pain, in a few short hours...' Between the telephone call from the nursing home in the afternoon to say that Alexander had developed a broncho-pneumonial infection and the call to say he had died, only a couple of hours elapsed.

'I felt guilty at not having rushed down, at not having seen him since my return from Italy... And then a sense of anguish, almost panic, began to take over. It was like something from childhood.'

'...'

'Yes, like childhood,' I repeat.

'Perhaps,' he begins tentatively, 'you're also re-living his earlier loss...'

'The rage I feared had made him leave?'

'And the anguish and guilt you felt about him leaving...'

'Yes...' With the uncertainty of a faded sepia photograph, a memory floats up of myself standing alone in the hall waiting for him to come down the stairs, in his khaki kilt, and get into the car . . . to leave – for how long? for ever? – to fight against the Germans, the Nazis . . . Ilse . . . Janey . . .

'Uh-huh . . . ' After a while, he continues: 'I was wondering whether as a child you didn't simultaneously take in and reject many of your father's attitudes.'

'Why accept them if I rejected them?'

'Because he was your father, on the one hand. Because he was tyrannical, on the other . . . '

'Ah! . . . We had so many things in common that we never shared. Our faults . . . '

' . . . '

'I couldn't . . . ' Or wouldn't, I thought, as the sun came out again and the graveyard grass shone after the shower of rain. It was a simple service in a small country church. Villagers, their faces reverently mournful, came to offer condolences. In his twenty years of retirement here he had been well-liked. We formed a ragged procession: my half-sister and half-brother, Alexander's oldest children from his first marriage, whom I barely know; Colin, who had flown from Rome, our sons, my daughter . . . The Somerset hills were soft and green, the smell of cows from the field beyond lay heavy on the air . . .

'There was a sense of profound tranquility. It was a good place to be laid to rest,' I said. 'During the brief ceremony I felt not sadness but longing . . . '

' . . . '

'I'm not sure what I longed for. To be with him, somehow, I think.'

'The longing for the father you lost . . . '

'Yes. Or to be at peace with him.' There's a silence, then I say: 'In destroying him I destroyed something in myself. I had no "I" for him.'

I hear him move in his chair. For a time, as though waiting for me, he says nothing. But I'm silent.

'I'm reminded,' he says at last, 'of a child analyst who wrote, paraphrasing Freud, that the ego is a graveyard scattered with the headstones of lost objects . . . So yours is of many origins: your mother, father, Ilse, Bert . . . '

'Too many,' I say, 'all fractured. I never tried to make anything of those littered tombstones.'

'It's all the more difficult when you don't know whom you're building it for.'

'I had a different "I" for each of them . . . It's the original split.'

'Yes,' he says, 'your father and mother weren't united in what they wanted of you. Then your father left, they separated, and you didn't have a second chance in adolescence . . . '

Standing by the graveside I thought, there's still a chance, it's not too late. Writing is a way of recuperating what has been lost.

'Perhaps you want to make some reparation for the guilt you felt as a child.'

'For wanting to destroy him so I could have my mother to myself?'

'Uh-huh . . . '

'And for wanting to destroy her . . . '

The silence seems endless. The phrases form and I hold them back until they're no longer containable:

'A monument to destruction – that's what I've wanted to make from all the bits of tombstones. A memorial glorifying the dead in me. How can one recreate the past if one is constantly destroying it?'

' . . . '

'No! I have to make good all those broken and scattered tombstones inside myself first.'

'You made a start recently with your return to the manor . . . '

'Ah yes . . . ' The dark hall where I stand anxiously waiting for my father to leave vanishes, and the new hall takes its place lightly and gracefully . . . 'Yes, I seem to have made my peace with the house.'

'Well, your people live on in you perhaps more than you want to believe. Your mother, father, Ilse . . . '

'Perhaps they do . . . ' In the inner darkness where I'm confined, where nothing now moves, I see myself looking back down at my childhood, as though through a glass funnel that narrows at the far end, and silently I feel them gathering, coming together, until they fill the emptiness around me, and in their eyes, unimaginably, I see an indestructible love, in their bodies touching each other, an unsurpassable assurance, and I stand there, my hands by my side, like a child overwhelmed with wonder . . .

'It was the unity of love you yearned for,' he says.

'Instead of the fragments, yes. The dead live on in us, despite everything, don't they? Like people in books whom you can return to time and again . . . '

'Sure.'

I rest in the silence; and then, from the wall of my mind, I sense doubt creeping like a nocturnal insect. 'But all we've done here is to pick up the bits every now and again. Examine the fragments. We've never seen the totality, the causal relationships between them.'

'I doubt that one can ever be so precise.'

I reflect for a time. 'I suppose it means learning to become one's own analyst, the analyst of oneself, then . . . '

'I'd say so, yes.'

But still, in the silence, there's a secret doubt. Finally, I voice it: 'I've always thought that history served one purpose at least. By discovering the major factors of change one could learn from them. The same ought to be true of an individual's history.'

'Yes . . . You want to be the subject of your history instead of the object you felt yourself to be,' he replies warmly.

'The subject, yes – but also the object. It's the synthesis of the two, isn't it?'

'The author of your childhood then, the historian of your past.'

'That's what I intend – to write about it from inside and out . . . '

'I'm sure . . . ' He pauses. 'Well, we'll have to leave it there for today.'

I find my glasses and swing my legs off the couch. 'I'll see you next Monday.' I turn to look at him for a moment, and his face is impassive.

Ronald Fraser was born in 1930 and educated in England, the United States, and Switzerland. He is the author of a novel published in England in 1960 and three oral histories: *In Hiding: The Life of Manuel Cortes* (1972); *Tajos: The Story of a Village on the Costa del Sol* (1973); and *Blood of Spain: An Oral History of the Spanish Civil War* (1979). He lives in London.